# KICK IT

Dr. Judy Rosenberg

# KICK IT

**Stop Smoking And Be The Cause®
Of Better Outcomes For Your Life**

**Dr. Judy Rosenberg**

**KICK IT: Stop Smoking And Be The Cause\* Of Better Outcomes For Your Life**
© 2026 by Dr. Judy Rosenberg

**Published by**
Noble Publishing House
United States of America

**Disclaimer**
The information contained in this book is intended for educational and informational purposes only. It is not intended to serve as a substitute for professional medical advice, diagnosis, or treatment. Smoking cessation can have medical implications, and readers should consult with a qualified healthcare provider before beginning any quit-smoking program, particularly if they have underlying health conditions, are pregnant, or are taking medications.

The psychological techniques and methods described in this book are based on Dr. Judy Rosenberg's clinical experience and are presented for self-help purposes. They are not intended to replace professional psychotherapy or counseling. If you are experiencing a mental health crisis, severe depression, or emotional distress, please seek immediate help from a licensed mental health professional or contact a crisis hotline.

Individual results may vary. The author and publisher make no guarantees regarding the outcomes of using the methods described herein and assume no responsibility or liability for any actions taken as a result of reading this book.

The case studies and patient stories in this book are composite examples based on the author's clinical experience. Names, identifying details, and circumstances have been changed to protect patient confidentiality.

**ISBN: 978-1-971451-00-8**
**Printing Information**
First edition
Printed in the United States of America

# FOREWORD

## Master Jun Chong
## Knows How to KICK IT!

" Control your mind.
Control your body. Control your habit. "

– Grand Master Jun Chong

Grand Master Jun Chong is a lifelong Tae Kwon Do practitioner whose teaching blends discipline, mindfulness, and personal accountability. With decades of experience training students of all ages—including Dr. Judy herself—Master Chong emphasizes that true strength begins with self-control of the body, the breath, and the mind. His philosophy extends beyond the mat, guiding students to break destructive habits, build resilience, and live with intention. Known for his calm authority and uncompromising integrity, Grand Master Chong teaches that mastery is not about domination, but about choosing clarity over impulse, every single day.

# ACKNOWLEDGEMENTS

Thank you Kevin Noble for all your brilliant editing and design work. You have been a major contributor to KICK IT!

To my children, grand children and our future generation: Never rely on a substance to substitute for true fulfillment which lies in human connection and a meaningful life.

-Dr. Judy Rosenberg

Dr. Judy Rosenberg

# CHAPTERS &
## PAGE NUMBERS.

# CHAPTER 1.

## WHY YOU REALLY SMOKE

### The Hidden Psychology Behind Your Addiction

> **If you have the why, you will figure out the how.**
> – Friedrich Nietzsche

# SARAH'S STORY

Sarah's hands trembled as she stepped outside her office building into the November wind. The million-dollar presentation she had just delivered should have been her proudest moment. Instead, she was desperate for a cigarette.

At thirty-eight, Sarah was an executive leading a thriving marketing team, a respected industry voice, and a devoted mother to her teenage daughter. She had it all. But one secret undermined everything. She was smoking nearly two packs a day.

When she caught her reflection in the office window, she didn't see a confident leader. Instead, she saw a woman negotiating multi-million-dollar contracts who couldn't go two hours without sneaking outside for a fix.

Sarah had tried everything—patches, gum, prescription medications, hypnosis, even cold-turkey attempts that lasted only days. Each failure deepened her shame and made her feel more hopeless.

What she didn't realize was that her struggle wasn't really about nicotine. The cigarette in her hand wasn't just delivering a chemical. It was delivering something far more personal. Something her fifteen-year-old self had once desperately needed but never received.

# MY NAME IS DR. JUDY ROSENBERG

I've spent more than four decades specializing in addiction, trauma, and emotional healing. I founded my first stop-smoking clinic, *Habit Breakers Inc.*, in my twenties. Since then, as a clinical psychologist, I've worked with thousands of patients—executives, teachers, nurses, construction workers, parents, and retirees. People from every walk of life.

What I discovered early on changed everything I thought I knew about addiction.

People don't smoke just because of nicotine. They smoke because cigarettes fill a psychological void, a "hole in the soul," created long before their first puff.

Sarah's story is an example of this. Once she understood what cigarettes had really been doing for her, everything changed. Eight months later she was smoke-free. She was calmer, more present, and no longer carrying the wound that had once made cigarettes feel essential.

# WHY I'M TELLING YOU THIS

If you're reading this, you may feel the way Sarah once did. Successful in other parts of life, but defeated by cigarettes. Maybe you've tried to quit more than once. Maybe you're hiding your smoking from people you love. Maybe you feel guilty about the example you're setting for your children. Or you're afraid of what smoking is doing to your health.

I want you to know something right now. You are not weak. You do not lack willpower. And you are not hopeless.

You've simply been trying to solve the wrong problem.

This book is going to show you how to solve the right one using the same clinical method I've refined through decades of practice.

# WHAT MAKES THIS DIFFERENT

Unlike motivational speakers or pop-psychology books, I'm a practicing clinical psychologist. These methods aren't based on pep talks or slogans. They come directly from the work I've done with patients facing the same struggles you are facing now.

- Every story you'll read comes from my practice (with names and details changed).
- Every technique has been tested in real sessions.
- Every insight has been proven with real people.

Most importantly, this book addresses the root cause of your addiction, not just the symptoms. We are going to heal the "hole in the soul" that cigarettes have been filling, so you won't need them anymore.

# SARAH'S TURNING POINT

When Sarah sat across from me in my office, she repeated the same line she had told herself for years.

"I don't understand why I can't just quit. I'm successful in every other area of my life. I run a team of twenty people, I just closed a multi-million dollar deal, but I can't stop smoking cigarettes. I can conquer literally anything but this."

She listed every method she had tried: nicotine patches that left her skin irritated, gum that made her jaw ache, medications that gave her vivid nightmares, and even a hypnotist who charged her $500. Nothing had worked for more than a few weeks.

So I asked her a different question. "Tell me about the first time you remember smoking."

Her answer revealed the truth.

"I was fifteen. My parents were going through a brutal divorce. My mom was crying all the time. My dad had moved out. I felt like I had to take care of everyone. My mother's tears, my younger siblings' fears, they were all on me. I stole cigarettes from my mom's purse and smoked them in my room. For the first time in months I felt calm. It was as if I could finally breathe again."

That cigarette wasn't about nicotine. It was about survival. It became her emotional pacifier. Her way of soothing feelings no one else could soothe.

Every quit attempt that relied on willpower alone was doomed because it ignored the wound underneath. Once we identified and healed that wound, everything shifted. She didn't have to force herself not to smoke. She simply didn't want to.

## THE HIDDEN PSYCHOLOGY BEHIND ADDICTION

In my decades of practice, I've seen this same pattern again and again. Nearly every smoker carries a story like Sarah's. Some disruption occurred in early attachment that left them feeling unsafe, unseen, or unsupported.

These experiences create negative core beliefs—deep-seated assumptions about the self and the world that become part of a person's psychological DNA. Beliefs such as:

- "I'm not important enough to come first."
- "I have to take care of everyone else's feelings."
- "I'm not safe unless I'm in control."
- "I'm not lovable unless I'm perfect."
- "I'm all alone and no one understands me."

Children with these beliefs instinctively find ways to self-soothe. Some turn to food. Some to personal or career achievement. Many, surrounded by prevalent smoking and vaping in our culture, turn to cigarettes or vape devices.

These devices don't just deliver nicotine. They deliver the illusion of being comforted, of being in control, of being enough. That's why quitting feels impossible. You're not just giving up a habit, you're also giving up your primary coping mechanism.

## YOUR JOURNEY THROUGH THIS BOOK

This book will guide you through the same process I use with my patients:

- **Part I: The Psychology of Smoking:** You'll uncover your "why," learn the Mind Map method, and identify your smoking personality.
- **Part II: The Clinical Method for Breaking Free:** You'll dismantle your defenses, experience the paradigm shift, and create a personalized quit plan.
- **Part III: Living in Freedom:** You'll prevent relapse, strengthen your new identity, and understand your multigenerational impact.

At the heart of this process is my patented Mind Map. It is a nine-panel framework that charts your journey from the original wound, through chaos and defense, into healing and freedom. This isn't theory. It's the same roadmap thousands of people have used to transform their lives.

## YOUR COMPELLING WHY

Here's what I tell every patient who comes into my office: if you don't have a compelling reason to quit, you're setting yourself up for failure.

"*I want to be healthier*" isn't compelling enough. Your unconscious mind doesn't care about abstract goals. It only cares about immediate needs and survival.

"*My doctor told me to quit*" also isn't enough. External pressure rarely creates lasting change. Countless times I've seen patients facing cancer or emphysema and still be unable to quit.

But when someone says, "*I want to break the cycle so my daughter never learns to handle stress by smoking*," that's compelling.

When they say, "*I want to reclaim my power from cigarettes and stop letting them dictate the outcomes of my life*," that's compelling.

When they say, "*I want to heal the wound that created my addiction so I can finally feel whole*," that's compelling.

Sarah eventually found her own compelling why: "***I want to show my daughter that there are healthy ways to cope with stress. I want to break the generational pattern of using substances to avoid feelings, and allow her to live the life she deserves.***"

That why carried her through cravings, doubts, and the fear of change.

What will be your compelling *why?*

# THE PROMISE OF TRANSFORMATION

I can't promise this journey will always feel easy. What I can promise is that it works when you address the root causes.

Here's what transformation looks like in practice:

- **You stop seeing cigarettes as your source of comfort.** You learn to comfort yourself in healthier ways—through self-compassion and connection with others.
- **You stop seeing cigarettes as your way to gain control over your life.** You discover that real control comes from inner strength, not from a paper tube filled with toxins.
- **You stop seeing cigarettes as your way to gain confidence.** You realize your authentic self is more powerful than any performance or image you tried to project with smoke.

This process is not about willpower. It's about healing the original wound so cigarettes lose their purpose. Once that happens, you don't have to grit your teeth through cravings. You simply don't want to smoke anymore.

That's what happened with Sarah.

# SARAH'S LIFE TODAY

Eight months after our first session, Sarah called me with an update I'll never forget.

"Dr. Judy, something amazing happened yesterday. My daughter came home from school stressed about a test. Instead of disappearing to my room or sneaking outside for a cigarette, I sat with her at the kitchen table. We talked through her anxiety together. I even taught her the breathing technique you showed me. For the first time, I was calm, present, and emotionally available. I was really there for her."

Sarah wasn't just smoke-free. She was free. Free from the shame of hiding. Free from the constant mental energy spent managing her addiction. Free from the barrier that had always stood between her and her daughter.

She had reclaimed her authentic power. And now she was passing that gift on to the next generation.

## THE DEEPER PSYCHOLOGY

Sarah's story highlights a truth I've seen in hundreds of patients. Cigarettes are never just about nicotine. They are about the feelings that were too heavy to handle as a child, the beliefs formed in those moments, and the coping mechanisms built on top of them.

That's why quitting often feels terrifying. You're not just setting down a pack of cigarettes. You're letting go of the very thing you've used for decades to regulate your emotions.

But here's the paradox: the thing that once helped you survive is now keeping you stuck. Cigarettes don't actually calm you or give you a sense of confidence or control. They create anxiety, dependence, and self-doubt. They steal credit for the comfort that you create on your own–from your own breath, your own nervous system, your own strength.

The day you see that clearly, everything changes.

## THE HIDDEN COST OF SMOKING

Most people already know cigarettes damage the body. They know about cancer, heart disease, emphysema. But the real trap is psychological.

Every time you light up, you reinforce a lie: that you can't handle life without smoke in your lungs. That lie keeps you stuck in what I call the Double Dungeon of Darkness. One door is the chemical addiction. The other is the belief that cigarettes are your lifeline. Both feel locked, so you stay in the dark.

But neither door is truly locked. Nicotine withdrawal is uncomfortable but temporary. And the psychological dependency—the belief that smoking is your coping mechanism—is based on illusions that collapse once you face them honestly.

Sarah learned this. Thousands of others have too. And you can as well.

## YOU ARE NOT HOPELESS

If you've tried and failed before, you may be tempted to think you'll never succeed. Many of my patients walked into my office carrying that same belief. They had tried patches, gum, medications, and sheer willpower, and nothing lasted. They thought something was wrong with them.

But the truth is, nothing was wrong with them. They just hadn't been shown how to heal the wound underneath the smoking. Once they did, everything shifted.

This book is your guide to making that same shift. You don't need superhuman willpower. You need understanding. You need tools that work with your psychology instead of against it. And you need to connect with a compelling "why" that makes cigarettes irrelevant.

## YOUR JOURNEY BEGINS HERE

As you move through the chapters ahead, you'll learn how to:

- Identify the childhood wounds that created your smoking habit.
- Understand the defenses that have kept you stuck.
- Break through the illusions cigarettes have built.
- Experience the paradigm shift that makes smoking look repulsive instead of comforting.
- Build a new identity as someone who simply doesn't smoke.

This is not about deprivation. It's about freedom.

Sarah's story shows what happens when someone finally heals at the root. If it was possible for her, it's possible for you.

## A SIMPLE PRACTICE TO START RIGHT NOW

Before you turn the page, I want you to have something practical in your hands. One of the main reasons people smoke is because cigarettes appear to regulate breathing and calm the nervous system. But the truth is, it isn't the cigarette. It's the breathing.

Here's a clinical breathing technique I teach all my patients. It works immediately to calm the body and it gives you the same relief you thought you were getting from smoking, without the poison.

The **4-7-8 Breathing Technique:**

1. Exhale completely through your mouth.
2. Inhale gently through your nose for four counts.
3. Hold your breath for seven counts.
4. Exhale slowly through your mouth for eight counts.
5. Repeat three or four times.

Try it now. Pay attention to how quickly your body responds. Notice the tension in your shoulders easing. Notice how your thoughts slow down. You're proving to yourself that you already have healthier tools at your disposal.

This is just one of many practical methods you'll learn in this book. Each technique is designed to replace what cigarettes have been providing for you—calming effects, a sense of confidence or control—with real, authentic tools that support healing.

## PREPARING FOR DEEPER WORK

The breathing exercise is a bridge. It shows you that what cigarettes seemed to give you has always been available from within. But understanding this intellectually isn't enough. You need to uncover how cigarettes took root in your life in the first place.

That's where the next chapter begins.

You'll learn the full Mind Map framework—my patented nine-panel method for transformation. It will show you exactly how your smoking pattern was created, how it kept you trapped, and how to dismantle it at the root. You'll see where you are in the process right now and what steps will move you forward.

Before we go there, take a moment to reflect. The answers you come up with will prepare you for the deeper work ahead.

## REFLECTION QUESTIONS

1. What was happening in your life when you first started smoking regularly?
2. What feeling does smoking give you? Comfort, control, confidence, or something else?
3. When do you crave cigarettes most? During specific emotions, situations, or times of day?
4. If you're honest, what would you lose if you quit? Remember, your unconscious mind associates cigarettes with something valuable, even if it's an illusion.

Write your answers down. Don't just think about them. The act of putting your words on paper stimulates alternate synaptic pathways, creating clarity and preparing your mind for change.

# Question 1

What was happening in your
life when you first started
smoking?

_____

_____

_____

_____

_____

# Question 2

What feeling does smoking
give you? Comfort, control,
performance?

_____

_____

_____

_____

_____

# Question 3

When do you crave
cigarettes most? Time of day?
Situation?

_____

_____

_____

_____

_____

# Question 4

If you're honest, what would
you lose when you quit?

_____

_____

_____

_____

_____

# THE TRUTH ABOUT CIGARETTES

The cigarette has never been your friend. It's been your prison guard, disguised as a companion. It claimed to comfort you, but it kept you lonely. It promised control, but it made you dependent. It tried to project confidence, but it only deepened your insecurity.

That role ends now.

From this point forward, you are stepping into a process that will expose the cigarette for what it really is: a thief that has taken enough of your time, health, and energy.

# YOUR JOURNEY INTO THE MIND MAP

In the next chapter, you'll see the complete framework that maps the path from addiction to freedom. The Mind Map will help you understand not just what you've been doing, but why you've been doing it, and most importantly, how to heal.

You'll see how childhood wounds shaped your beliefs, how those beliefs created defense mechanisms, and how those defenses locked you in. You'll also see how the process of healing works, panel by panel, until freedom becomes your new normal.

Your healing journey begins with understanding. And understanding begins with the Mind Map.

# MY CLOSING MESSAGE TO YOU

Before you turn the page, I want you to sit with one thought. You didn't start smoking because you were weak. You started smoking because you were resourceful. You were a child or a teenager trying to cope with something bigger than you could handle at the time. Cigarettes became your solution, not your failure.

Now you are an adult. You have new resources, new awareness, and new tools. You no longer need cigarettes to survive. You're ready to heal the original wound instead of covering it over with nicotine.

Sarah's story is an example of this. Once she understood what cigarettes had really been doing for her, everything changed. Eight months later she was smoke-free. She was calmer, more present, and no longer carrying the wound that had once made cigarettes feel essential.

This is not about losing something. It's about gaining yourself back. Let's begin.

# CHAPTER 2.

## THE BE THE CAUSE®: MIND MAP

### Your Clinical Roadmap from Addiction to Freedom

> " The cave you fear to enter holds the treasure you seek. "
>
> – Joseph Campbell

# WHY THE MIND MAP MATTERS

When I began my clinical work in the 1980s, I was puzzled by a pattern I couldn't ignore. Patients would come to me desperate to quit smoking. They would make it through the first few days of nicotine withdrawal, sometimes even weeks. But again and again, more than 90 percent relapsed.

It didn't matter if they were using patches, gum, or pure willpower. Even the most determined patients would eventually return to cigarettes. The question haunted me: *why?*

The answer became clear after years of listening closely to their stories. Smoking was never just about nicotine. It was about emotional wounds, core beliefs, and survival strategies formed in childhood.

I needed a way to help patients see this clearly. That's when I developed the Be The Cause® Mind Map. It's a nine-panel roadmap that reveals exactly how addictions form, how they trap us, and how we can break free.

The Mind Map has since guided thousands of people through transformation. It shows you where you are in your journey and, more importantly, what steps will move you forward. It's a proven clinical framework that has helped patients heal at the deepest level.

# THE NINE PANELS AT A GLANCE

The Mind Map is organized into three stages, each with three panels. You can picture it as a grid of nine squares.

### Stage 1: Encoding

- **Panel 1: Wounds** – the original emotional injury.
- **Panel 2: Reactions** – how you coped with the wound.
- **Panel 3: Encoding** – the core beliefs you carried forward.

### Stage 2: Decoding

- **Panel 4: Chaos** – the problems created by your old patterns.
- **Panel 5: Defenses** – the excuses and justifications that protect your smoking.
- **Panel 6: Breakdown/Breakthrough** – the choice point between staying stuck or healing.

### Stage 3: Recoding

- **Panel 7: Paradigm Shift** – seeing smoking through new eyes.
- **Panel 8: New Encoding** – building new beliefs and behaviors.
- **Panel 9: Unity and Service** – living free and passing the healing forward.

# MIND MAP™

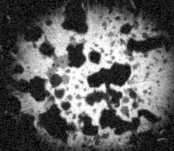
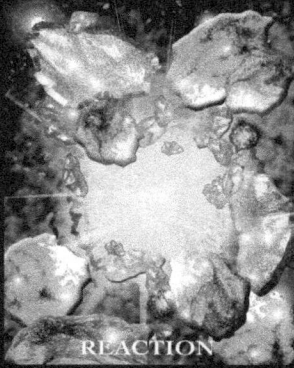
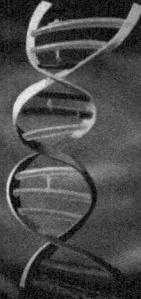

WOUND  REACTION  ENCODING

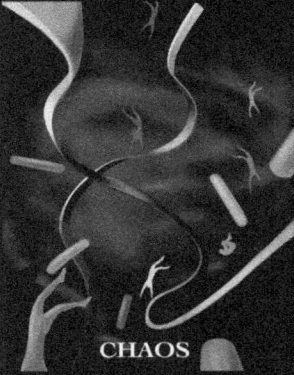
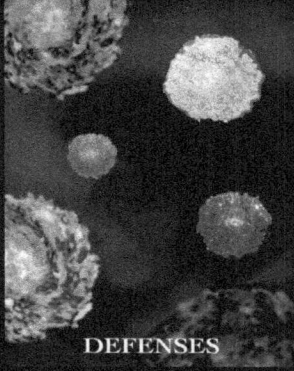

CHAOS  DEFENSES  BREAKDOWN/ BREAKTHROUGH

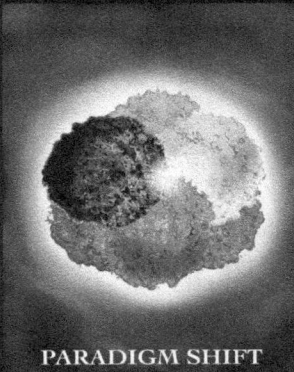
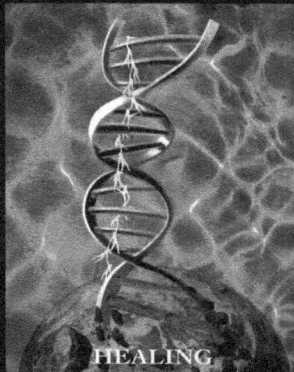
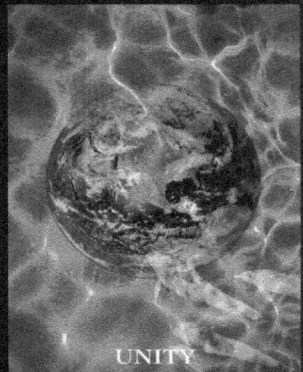

PARADIGM SHIFT  HEALING  UNITY

Be The Cause®
Healing Human Disconnect®
www.psychologicalhealingcenter.com

The Mind Map takes you from fragmentation to wholeness, from addiction to freedom. It's a guide that shows not only what you've been through, but how to move into lasting transformation.

## MARCUS'S STORY

Let me show you how the Mind Map works by introducing Marcus.

Marcus was a 42-year-old emergency room nurse. His life looked steady from the outside. He was respected at work, dedicated to his family, and committed to his patients. But behind the scenes, Marcus was sneaking away to smoke between shifts, hiding his habit from coworkers and especially from his teenage son.

One night, his son confronted him directly. "Dad, how can you spend all day saving people's lives, but still smoke? Don't you care about your own?"

The words landed like a shock. Marcus could tell his excuses were running out. He felt like a fraud, teaching others about health for his career while secretly destroying his own.

# STAGE 1: ENCODING

## Panel 1 - The Wound

When Marcus and I began working together, we started with his earliest memories.

"I remember being maybe seven years old," he told me. "Kids at school made fun of me. I came home crying. My mom just said, 'Don't let them bother you.' My dad told me to 'toughen up.' I learned pretty quickly that my feelings were my own problem."

This is what I call the wound. It doesn't always look like trauma from the outside. Marcus's parents weren't cruel. They provided food, shelter, and education. But emotionally, they weren't present. They didn't know how to comfort him or validate his inner world.

That gap—between what a child needs and what they actually receive—is enough to create a wound that lingers for decades.

## Panel 2 - The Reaction

Children don't have the maturity to understand why their needs aren't met. They just know they hurt. So they come up with coping strategies.

Marcus's reaction was what I call "hyper-responsibility." He stopped looking for comfort and instead became the caretaker.

At ten years old, he had already begun suppressing his own emotions. Marcus constantly checked in on his mom when she looked sad or tried to cheer up his dad after work.

By adolescence, Marcus had learned that his role in life was to manage everyone else's feelings while ignoring his own. He became the "little adult," mature beyond his years but carrying a secret loneliness.

## Panel 3 – The Encoding

Over time, the wound and the reaction hardened into a core belief:

> *"I'm only valuable when I'm taking care of others. My feelings don't matter, and I have to handle my own stress alone."*

At sixteen, Marcus discovered cigarettes. They seemed to provide exactly what he had been missing.

"Smoking was the first thing I found that was just for me," he explained. "It was five minutes where I didn't have to take care of anyone else. I could just breathe."

Cigarettes became his substitute parent—always available, never judging, always providing a false sense of comfort.

That's how the encoding stage works. A childhood wound creates a reaction. That reaction morphs into a belief. And that belief sets the stage for addiction.

## WHY THIS MATTERS

By the time Marcus reached adulthood, cigarettes had become more than just a habit. They were woven into his identity.

To quit smoking wasn't just to give up nicotine. It was to give up the only tool he believed he had for soothing himself.

This is why traditional quit methods fail. They tell people to give up cigarettes without addressing the emotional wounds underneath. Without healing that root, the habit returns.

The Mind Map changes that. By seeing where you are in the nine panels, you gain clarity. You understand what cigarettes are really doing for you and what they're taking from you. Most importantly, you discover how to replace them with something real.

# STAGE 2: DECODING

Once our wounds and their core beliefs are encoded, life eventually brings situations that stress those patterns to their breaking point. That's what **Stage 2** is about. The old ways of coping stop working, and the cracks begin to show.

## Panel 4 – Chaos

By his early forties, Marcus's life looked successful. He had a steady job, a family who loved him, and the respect of colleagues. But under the surface, chaos was building.

His teenage son had begun questioning him about smoking. His wife worried about his health and noticed he was winded after long shifts. At work, the physical demands of being an ER nurse were becoming harder to manage.

"I started feeling like a hypocrite," Marcus admitted. "I'd tell patients about the dangers of smoking while sneaking out back for a cigarette between patients. I felt like I was living two different lives."

Chaos isn't punishment. It's information. It's your psyche's way of saying, "The old patterns aren't working anymore. Something deeper has to change."

For Marcus, chaos meant he could no longer pretend cigarettes were harmless breaks. The contradictions in his life were catching up with him.

## Panel 5 – Defense Mechanisms

When chaos gets too loud, most people don't immediately change. Instead, the mind activates defenses—psychological bodyguards that protect us from facing the full weight of our wounds.

Marcus used several of the classic defenses I've seen in my practice:

- **Rationalization**: "I only smoke during really stressful shifts."
- **Minimization**: "I don't smoke as much as other people. It's just a few cigarettes a day."
- **Isolation**: "I never smoke around my son or at work. I keep it separate."
- **Denial**: "I could quit anytime I want. I just don't want to deal with the stress right now."

These defenses aren't random excuses. They're survival tools. At some point, they protected Marcus from feelings he couldn't handle. But now they were his prison guards. They allowed him to maintain the illusion of control while the addiction deepened.

The crack came when his son looked him in the eye and said, "Dad, don't you care about your own life?" Suddenly the defenses rang hollow. Marcus couldn't explain his smoking to a teenager because he could barely explain it to himself.

## Panel 6 – Breakdown or Breakthrough

This is the most critical panel in the Mind Map. It's the turning point.

Panel 6 is when your defenses stop working. You face a choice:

Retreat into breakdown by strengthening your defenses and sinking deeper into chaos.

Or step into breakthrough by allowing yourself to confront the wounds underneath.

Marcus hit his Panel 6 moment that night with his son. "I realized I couldn't keep pretending cigarettes were just a little habit," he said. "I had to admit they were controlling me. And I hated that."

Breakthrough begins when you stop managing symptoms and start addressing the root. It can feel terrifying—like the ground is shifting beneath your feet—but it's also the doorway to real transformation.

## THE CHOICE POINT

I've seen patients take both paths at Panel 6. Some retreat to *Panel 5—Defense Mechanisms* by rationalizing harder, hiding their smoking more carefully, or convincing themselves they'll quit "someday."

Others break through by admitting the defenses aren't working and instead choose to begin the deeper work of healing.

The difference is usually support. People who face Panel 6 alone often collapse back into old patterns. Those with guidance, encouragement, or a clear framework are able to push forward.

That's why the Mind Map is so powerful. It gives you a structure to hold onto when your defenses crumble. It helps you see that the fear you feel is actually a sign of progress.

# HOW TO RECOGNIZE PANEL 6 IN YOURSELF

You'll know you're approaching Panel 6 if:

- Your usual justifications for smoking start sounding false, even to you.
- You feel unusually emotional or vulnerable.
- You begin questioning more than just your smoking—other parts of your life feel unstable too.
- You feel hopeful about change and terrified of failure at the same time.
- You notice how much energy smoking actually takes to manage.

These are not signs of weakness. They are signs that your defenses are weakening, and healing is becoming possible.

# MARCUS'S BREAKTHROUGH

For Marcus, the breakthrough came gradually after his son's confrontation. In our sessions, he began admitting things he had never said aloud.

"I used to tell myself cigarettes calmed me down," he said. "But when I think about it, I was more anxious as a smoker than I am now. I was always worrying. Do I have enough cigarettes? When will I get my next break? Who might catch me?"

He paused, then added: "The cigarettes weren't calming me. They were running my life."

That realization was his breakthrough. The illusion cracked. For the first time, Marcus saw smoking for what it really was: not a comfort, but a trap.

# WHY PANEL 6 IS SO POWERFUL

Every patient I've worked with reaches a version of this moment. It's painful, but it's also liberating.

When you let your defenses crack, you finally face the truth. Cigarettes don't soothe you. They don't make you stronger. They don't make life easier. They only cover wounds that are waiting to be healed.

Panel 6 is where courage and healing meet. It's the place where breakdown can turn into breakthrough.

# STAGE 3: RECODING

When you reach Panel 6 and choose breakthrough over breakdown, something powerful begins to happen. The old illusions collapse. You see cigarettes differently. This is **Stage 3** of the Mind Map—the process of building a new identity where smoking simply doesn't fit.

## Panel 7 - The Paradigm Shift

The Paradigm Shift is the moment when perception flips. What once looked like relief now looks like poison. What once felt necessary now feels unnecessary.

I call this the "A-Ha Moment." It doesn't always come like a lightning bolt. For some, it's gradual. But the shift is unmistakable:

- Cigarettes taste like ash instead of providing comfort.
- You no longer think "I'm trying not to smoke." You simply think "I don't smoke."
- You realize the calm you thought came from nicotine was always coming from your own breath.

Marcus experienced his paradigm shift one afternoon at work. A trauma patient came into the ER, and for the first time in years, he realized he wasn't thinking about cigarettes. He was calm, focused, and present without them. "It hit me," he said. "I didn't need cigarettes to manage stress. I had been giving them credit for my own strength."

## Panel 8 - New Encoding

Once your perception changes, the work becomes about reinforcement. You build new beliefs, emotions, and behaviors that match your smoke-free identity.

For Marcus, this meant:

- Practicing meditation during breaks instead of sneaking outside.
- Talking openly with his wife about his stress instead of hiding it.
- Asking colleagues for support instead of pretending he was fine.

This is what Panel 8 is about. It's the creation of new "psychological DNA." Old beliefs like "I have to handle stress alone" are replaced with new beliefs like "I deserve support and connection."

The more you practice these new patterns, the more automatic they become.

## Panel 9 - Unity and Service

The final panel represents integration. You don't just live smoke-free—you thrive in it—and often, you find yourself wanting to help others.

Marcus reached this stage eight months after quitting. He was mentoring younger nurses, advocating for employee wellness, and modeling health for his son. "I don't even think of myself as a smoker who quit," he told me. "I'm just someone who doesn't smoke."

That's the essence of Panel 9. Your healing becomes part of something larger.

# THE NEUROSCIENCE OF TRANSFORMATION

Everything I've described isn't just psychology. It's also neuroscience.

Your brain wires itself based on repeated experiences. Years of smoking created neural highways that made cigarettes feel like survival. That's why quitting felt impossible. Your brain had been trained to expect nicotine as a solution.

But here's the hopeful truth: the brain is plastic. It can change at any age. Every time you practice a healthy coping strategy instead of smoking, you carve a new pathway. Every time you breathe deeply or reach out for support, you reinforce that path.

Over time, the old smoking circuits weaken from disuse. The new ones grow stronger. This is called neuroplasticity—the brain's ability to rewire itself.

It means transformation isn't just possible. It's inevitable when you practice the right patterns.

# WHY THE MIND MAP WORKS

Traditional smoking cessation methods fail because they focus on symptoms, not causes.

- Nicotine replacement therapy gives you the drug without addressing why you needed it in the first place.
- Medications can block nicotine receptors, but they can't heal childhood wounds.
- Hypnosis might suggest you are a non-smoker, but it doesn't change the beliefs buried in your unconscious.
- Willpower alone asks you to resist something your mind believes is essential for

survival.

The Mind Map succeeds because it goes deeper. When you heal the original wound, cigarettes lose their purpose. You don't have to force yourself not to smoke, you simply don't want to anymore.

That's why Marcus succeeded. That's why Sarah succeeded. And that's why hundreds of my patients have stayed smoke-free for good.

## WHERE ARE YOU RIGHT NOW?

Most readers find themselves somewhere in **Panels 4-6**. You've experienced enough chaos to know something has to change. Your defenses are starting to crack. You may even be at your own breakdown/breakthrough moment.

That's not a bad place to be. It's actually the ideal place to begin this process. The discomfort you feel isn't proof that you're broken. It's proof that you're ready.

## REFLECTION QUESTIONS

Before moving to the next chapter, take a few minutes to reflect. Write or type your answers down below.

# Question 1

What was happening in your family when you first started smoking?

_____

_____

_____

_____

# Question 2

What emotional needs were unmet in your childhood?

_____

_____

_____

_____

## Question 3

What core belief might you have
carried forward from that time?

_____
_____
_____
_____
_____

## Question 4

Which panel of the Mind Map
feels most like where you are
today?

_____
_____
_____
_____

These questions aren't about judgment. They're about awareness. Once you see where you are on the map, you can see the path forward.

## PREPARING FOR CHAPTER 3: YOUR SMOKING PERSONALITY

Now that you've got the Mind Map down, it's time to make this personal. In Chapter 3, you're going to uncover the three smoking personalities: Comfort, Control, and Performance. One of them will feel like it's describing you to a T.

Why does that matter? Because once you know your smoking personality, you stop treating this like a generic habit and start understanding your psychology. That's the key.

From there, we can build a quit plan that doesn't just fight the addiction—it's built around you.

# CHAPTER 3.

## YOUR SMOKING PERSONA

### Understanding Your Unique Path To Freedom

**" Know Thyself "**

– Ancient Greek Aphorism

# WHY YOUR SMOKING PERSONALITY MATTERS

The Mind Map™ framework applies to everyone, but how you smoke—and why—depends on your personal psychology. In my decades of practice, I've noticed three distinct smoking personalities. These patterns don't just explain why you reach for a cigarette. They also reveal the challenges you'll face when quitting, and the tools that will work best for you.

Some people smoke to calm emotions. Others smoke to stay in control. Still others smoke to feel confident or to perform socially. Each type is shaped by childhood experiences, core beliefs, and coping strategies that began long before the first cigarette.

Once you recognize your smoking personality, quitting no longer feels random or overwhelming. You can finally see the logic behind your habit and the clear path out of it.

# THE THREE TYPES OF SMOKERS

Over the years I've identified three main "smoking personalities." Recognizing your type is crucial, because each is driven by different needs.

### The Comfort Smoker

- Uses cigarettes for emotional soothing.
- Grew up with emotionally unavailable caregivers.
- Smokes when stressed, lonely, or overwhelmed.
- Cigarettes act like a pacifier—a substitute for comfort they couldn't ask for or receive.

### THE CONTROL SMOKER

- Smokes to manage anxiety and create the illusion of control.
- Grew up in chaotic or unpredictable environments.
- Smokes before meetings, during conflicts, or whenever life feels unstable.
- Believes cigarettes bring clarity or calm.

### THE PERFORMANCE SMOKER

- Smokes for social confidence or creative "edge."
- Grew up with conditional love or pressure to achieve.
- Smokes during networking events, creative work, or public performances.
- Uses cigarettes as a prop for confidence or sophistication.

Most people recognize themselves right away in one of these categories. Some see traits of more than one. Either way, understanding your type is the first step toward breaking free. Next, we'll go into each type in more detail. If you immediately know your type, skip ahead and read the longer breakdown. If you feel you identify with multiple—or simply want to expand your awareness—read the ones you feel apply to you.

# THE COMFORT SMOKER: SEEKING SOOTHING AND SAFETY

- **Core Wound**: Emotional neglect or unavailability from caregivers
- **Core Belief**: "I'm alone. I have to take care of myself."
- **What Cigarettes Provide**: Comfort, self-soothing, emotional regulation.

## JENNIFER'S STORY

Jennifer, a 34-year-old registered nurse and mother of two, came to see me after her eight-year-old daughter asked a piercing question: "Mommy, why do you always go outside when you're sad?"

Jennifer's childhood looked stable from the outside. Her father was a hardworking teacher. Her mother kept the household running while working part-time as a bookkeeper. There was no chaos, no obvious abuse. But what was missing was emotional connection.

"I remember bringing home a drawing from school," Jennifer told me. "I wanted my mom to notice. She said, 'That's nice, honey, put it on the refrigerator.' Another time I cried because friends were excluding me at school. My dad just told me to focus on schoolwork. They weren't cruel. They just didn't know how to respond to feelings."

This is what I call **emotional invisibility**. Jennifer wasn't harmed by neglect in the physical sense, but her inner world was rarely seen or validated. Over time, she formed the belief: "My emotions don't really matter. I have to handle them on my own."

By sixteen, Jennifer discovered cigarettes. They felt like her first private comfort. "When I smoked," she said, "it was like I finally mattered to myself. For those few minutes, I felt less invisible."

## HOW COMFORT SMOKERS USE CIGARETTES

If you're a Comfort Smoker, cigarettes serve as your emotional pacifier. You probably smoke most often when you feel:

- Overwhelmed or stressed
- Lonely or disconnected from others
- Sad, anxious, or emotionally triggered
- Worn out from taking care of everyone else
- Drained after conflict or confrontation

For Comfort Smokers, the ritual is almost as powerful as the nicotine. The deep inhale, the pause, the hand-to-mouth motion—all mimic the rhythm of comfort. In those moments, the cigarette feels like a surrogate parent: always there, always "listening."

But here's the trap. While cigarettes appear to provide comfort, they actually reinforce isolation. Instead of seeking real support, Comfort Smokers withdraw further. The loneliness deepens, which fuels the cycle even more.

## THE COMFORT SMOKER'S MIND MAP JOURNEY

**Panels 1-3 (Encoding):** The wound is emotional neglect. The reaction is self-reliance. The encoding is the belief that "I have to handle my own feelings."

**Panels 4-6 (Decoding):** Life becomes overwhelming—stress at work, relationship challenges, parenting demands. The usual coping mechanism (smoking) starts to feel inadequate, but defenses kick in: "I only smoke when I'm stressed. It's not that much."

**Panels 7-9 (Recoding):** Healing happens when Comfort Smokers learn to accept support, practice self-compassion, and build genuine relationships. Cigarettes are no longer needed because real comfort replaces the illusion.

## PRACTICAL SIGNS YOU'RE A COMFORT SMOKER

- You crave cigarettes most when you feel emotionally unsettled.
- Smoking feels like "me time" in a life of giving to others.
- You hide your sadness or stress but smoke when you feel it.
- You describe cigarettes as a "friend" or "companion."

- You say things like, "I deserve this break," or "It's the only thing that relaxes me."

## HOW COMFORT SMOKERS HEAL

Breaking free requires replacing cigarettes with real sources of comfort. That means:

- **Building support systems.** Create a short list of people you can call when you need emotional connection. Practice reaching out.
- **Practicing self-compassion.** Learn to treat yourself kindly in moments of stress. Try a simple mantra: "This is hard, and I deserve care right now."
- **Creating soothing rituals.** Replace smoke breaks with grounding practices—herbal tea, journaling, or gentle breathing.
- **Letting yourself be seen.** Share feelings honestly with trusted people. Notice how real connection calms you more than smoking ever could.

Jennifer discovered this in therapy. She practiced calling a friend when she felt down instead of reaching for cigarettes. She created a bedtime ritual with her children that gave her the emotional closeness she had been missing. Bit by bit, the old belief that she was "invisible" began to dissolve.

She still had cravings early on, but over time, she noticed something surprising. "When I let myself cry, or when someone hugged me, the urge to smoke disappeared. It wasn't about nicotine at all. It was about wanting to feel cared for."

## DOES THIS SOUND LIKE YOU?

If you relate strongly to Jennifer's story, you may be a Comfort Smoker. That doesn't mean you're doomed to struggle. It means your healing path is clear: you'll succeed when you learn to comfort yourself authentically and allow others to comfort you too.

# THE CONTROL SMOKER: MANAGING ANXIETY AND OVERWHELM

- **Core Wound**: Chaos, unpredictability, or trauma in childhood
- **Core Belief**: "The world isn't safe. I must stay in control."
- **What Cigarettes Provide**: Calm, clarity, a sense of control

# DAVID'S STORY

David, a 41-year-old financial advisor, came to me convinced that cigarettes were the only thing keeping him steady. "They help me think straight," he explained. "When I'm under pressure, smoking gives me clarity."

But David's relationship with cigarettes didn't start in the boardroom. It began much earlier, in a childhood defined by unpredictability.

"My dad was an alcoholic," David told me. "I never knew who was walking through the door at night. Happy dad, angry dad, or passed-out dad. It was like living in a minefield. I learned to control whatever I could. My grades, my behavior, even the noise level in the house. But inside, I was always anxious."

By the time David reached business school, cigarettes felt like a lifeline. "During exams or big presentations, they gave me focus. I thought, if I smoke, I can handle it."

# HOW CONTROL SMOKERS USE CIGARETTES

If you're a Control Smoker, you probably reach for cigarettes when:

- You're facing high-pressure situations or important decisions.
- You feel overwhelmed by responsibilities.
- You're preparing for difficult conversations or conflicts.
- You need to concentrate or think through complex problems.
- You want to manage worry or perfectionist tendencies.

Control Smokers often describe cigarettes as their "reset button." The act of stepping outside, taking deep breaths, and focusing on the ritual creates a false sense of order. It feels like the one controllable factor in a chaotic or stressful world.

But the relief is temporary. Over time, smoking actually increases anxiety. David admitted he spent more mental energy managing his smoking than managing his clients' portfolios. "I was always calculating: do I have enough cigarettes, when's my next break, what if someone notices the smell? It was exhausting."

# THE CONTROL SMOKER'S MIND MAP JOURNEY

**Panels 1-3 (Encoding):** The wound is chaos or unpredictability. The reaction is hypervigilance and control-seeking. The encoding is the belief: "If I don't control everything, bad things will happen."

**Panels 4-6 (Decoding):** Life events—stress, health scares, relationship struggles—create chaos that cigarettes can't actually solve. Defenses rise: "I only smoke when it's really stressful. It helps me focus." Eventually the defenses fail, and the system breaks down.

**Panels 7-9 (Recoding):** Healing comes from learning to tolerate uncertainty, developing healthier ways to manage anxiety, and realizing that true control comes from inner stability rather than an external substance.

# PRACTICAL SIGNS YOU'RE A CONTROL SMOKER

· You crave cigarettes most when you feel anxious, pressured, or unprepared.

· You see cigarettes as helping you think clearly or regain focus.

· You smoke before important tasks, not just when you're bored or lonely.

· You describe smoking as "my way to stay in control".

· You get irritated if circumstances prevent you from smoking when you want to.

# HOW CONTROL SMOKERS HEAL

Breaking free means building tolerance for uncertainty and learning that your strength doesn't come from cigarettes—it comes from you. **Strategies include:**

· **Anxiety management skills.** Practice techniques like the **4-7-8 breathing technique** (inhale for 4 counts, hold for 7, exhale 8) to calm your nervous system.

· **Uncertainty practice.** Deliberately allow small moments of unpredictability like taking a new route to work or trying something without planning every detail. Teach yourself that you can handle the unknown.

· **Cognitive reframing.** Notice catastrophic thoughts ("If this meeting goes badly, I'll fail") and replace them with balanced ones ("I've handled challenges before; I can handle this too").

· **Control inventory.** List situations in your past where you managed stress without smoking. Remind yourself that cigarettes weren't the source of your strength—you were.

David used these tools consistently. Instead of smoking before meetings, he practiced three rounds of **4-7-8 breathing**. He learned to name his fears out loud to a colleague or to his wife, instead of bottling them up. Slowly, he discovered he could stay calm without lighting up.

"The cigarettes weren't giving me control," he realized. "They were controlling me. Once I stopped, I finally felt in charge of my own life again."

## DOES THIS SOUND LIKE YOU?

If David's story resonates, you may be a Control Smoker. That doesn't mean you're doomed to constant anxiety. It means your path to healing involves proving to yourself that you can live with uncertainty and still thrive.

Cigarettes don't give you control. They give you the illusion of control while quietly taking it away. When you build inner stability, you no longer need the illusion.

## THE PERFORMANCE SMOKER: MANAGING IMAGE AND SOCIAL ANXIETY

- **Core Wound:** Conditional love or high expectations
- **Core Belief**: "I'm only worthy if I perform."
- **What Cigarettes Provide**: Confidence, creativity, social acceptance.

## SHOSHANNAH'S STORY

Shoshannah was a 29-year-old marketing creative working at a health-conscious tech company. From the outside, she looked like a rising star: stylish, successful, and brimming with ideas. But behind the polished image, she was sneaking trips to the bathroom and parking lot to hit her nicotine vape, terrified her colleagues would discover her secret.

"The strange thing," Shoshannah admitted, "is that I don't vape all the time—only before big presentations, networking events, or when I'm trying to come up with new ideas. It feels like the vape pen helps me be the version of myself that everyone expects me to be."

Shoshannah grew up in a family where achievement meant approval. Her parents loved her, but love was tied to grades, awards, and performance. "I was the kid who had to get straight A's, play piano recitals, and join every sports team and club," she said. "It felt like I had to be successful to be loved."

Cigarettes entered her life in college. Surrounded by other creatives and intellectuals, she noticed how smoking made her feel sophisticated, confident, and just a little rebellious. "It became part of my persona," Shoshannah recalled. "The edgy, creative professional with a cigarette in hand.

"As I progressed through my career," she continued, "the smell of cigarrette smoke became problematic, so I switched to vapes. And I find myself relying upon it even more because the access to it is so easy, and it's so easy to mask."

## HOW PERFORMANCE SMOKERS USE CIGARETTES

If you're a Performance Smoker, cigarettes act as your confidence booster and social prop. You may smoke:

- Before giving a presentation or performance.
- During creative work or brainstorming sessions.
- In social situations to ease anxiety.
- To project sophistication, maturity, or control.
- To silence imposter syndrome.

Performance Smokers often say cigarettes help them "get into character." They describe smoking as part of their identity in specific roles—artist, executive, social connector—even if they don't smoke heavily outside of those roles.

But here's the trap. Cigarettes don't create confidence or special abilities. They mask insecurity. They give the illusion of ease while eroding authenticity. Shoshannah eventually realized she felt like a fraud, both for smoking in secret and for relying on a prop to feel capable.

## THE PERFORMANCE SMOKER'S MIND MAP JOURNEY

**Panels 1-3 (Encoding)**: The wound is conditional love. The reaction is striving and perfectionism. The encoding is the belief: "I'm only valuable when I impress others."

**Panels 4-6 (Decoding)**: Pressure builds in work and social settings. Cigarettes become the "go-to" for performance anxiety. Defenses emerge: "It's just part of the creative process. I don't smoke that much." Defenses can sustain temporarily—sometimes indefinitely— but eventually break you down over time.

**Panels 7-9 (Recoding)**: Healing begins when Performance Smokers separate their worth from their achievements. Authenticity replaces performance. Cigarettes are no longer needed when real self-confidence grows.

# PRACTICAL SIGNS YOU'RE A PERFORMANCE SMOKER

- You smoke most in social or professional settings, not when you're alone.
- You describe cigarettes as helping you feel confident, creative, or sophisticated.
- You smoke more during high-stakes events (presentations, deadlines, parties).
- You feel conflicted—cigarettes seem to enhance your image but also threaten it.
- You think of smoking as part of a persona, not just a habit.

# HOW PERFORMANCE SMOKERS HEAL

Healing means learning that real confidence doesn't come from cigarettes. It comes from authenticity. Strategies include:

- **Values clarification**: Before a performance or social event, remind yourself of your core values. Let them guide your behavior instead of relying on cigarettes to play a role. A simple 30-60 second mindfulness pause—closing your eyes, breathing deeply, and repeating your values—can anchor you in the right mindset and strengthen your ability to make healthy choices.
- **Authenticity practice**: In low-stakes settings, practice being genuine instead of polished. Notice that people connect more with the real you.
- **Confidence building without props**: Develop skills and habits that build genuine confidence—public speaking classes, creative pursuits, or physical training.
- **Reframing creativity**: Recognize that cigarettes don't generate ideas. The pause, the space, and the breathing do. Create rituals that give you that same mental space without smoke.

Shoshannah discovered this through deliberate practice. Instead of smoking before brainstorming, she took short "creativity walks" outdoors. Instead of sneaking a cigarette before networking events, she practiced power poses and deep breathing.

Six months later, she was surprised to realize her creativity had actually improved. "I thought cigarettes were my muse," she said. "But they were really my cage. I'm more creative and more confident now because I'm not hiding."

# DOES THIS SOUND LIKE YOU?

If Shoshannah's story resonates, you may be a Performance Smoker. That doesn't mean you need cigarettes to succeed. It means you've been relying on them as a prop.

The truth is, your authentic self is more powerful than any image you could project. When you stop outsourcing confidence to cigarettes, you discover that you never needed them in the first place.

## MIXED TYPES AND EVOLUTION

Most people see themselves clearly in one of the three smoking personalities. But it's also common to have traits from more than one type.

- **Comfort-Control Mix**: Often develops in people who grew up in both emotional neglect and chaotic environments. Cigarettes soothe their feelings and provide a sense of order.

- **Control-Performance Mix**: Common among high achievers who feel both pressured to perform and anxious about outcomes. Cigarettes seem to sharpen their focus and polish their image.

- **Comfort-Performance Mix**: Often seen in people-pleasers who crave connection but also feel they have to "perform" to be accepted. Cigarettes are used both for self-soothing and for confidence.

Smoking personalities can also evolve over time. A Performance Smoker who started in college might shift into a Control Smoker as career pressures mount. A Comfort Smoker who quits for a while may relapse during a period of chaos and take on more Control traits.

The point is not to fit yourself neatly into a box. It's to recognize the patterns that drive your smoking so you can choose the right tools to heal, and most importantly, be able to adapt as your life changes around you.

# SMOKING PERSONALITY ASSESSMENT

Take a few minutes to complete this self-assessment. Be honest with your answers. Circle or mark the answer that best matches your experience. Then tally up the points of your responses accordingly:

- 1 = Strongly Disagree
- 2 = Disagree

- 3 = Neutral
- 4 = Agree
- 5 = Strongly Agree

## COMFORT SMOKER STATEMENTS

● **I smoke most often when I'm feeling overwhelmed or emotionally triggered.**

☐ Strongly Disagree ☐ Disagree ☐ Neutral ☐ Agree ☐ Strongly Agree

● **Cigarettes help me feel calm and soothed when I'm upset.**

☐ Strongly Disagree ☐ Disagree ☐ Neutral ☐ Agree ☐ Strongly Agree

● **I often smoke when I need a break from taking care of others.**

☐ Strongly Disagree ☐ Disagree ☐ Neutral ☐ Agree ☐ Strongly Agree

● **I started smoking during a time when I felt lonely or unsupported.**

☐ Strongly Disagree ☐ Disagree ☐ Neutral ☐ Agree ☐ Strongly Agree

● **The ritual of smoking feels as important as the nicotine itself.**

☐ Strongly Disagree ☐ Disagree ☐ Neutral ☐ Agree ☐ Strongly Agree

● **I have difficulty asking for emtional support from others.**

☐ Strongly Disagree ☐ Disagree ☐ Neutral ☐ Agree ☐ Strongly Agree

● **I smoke more during relationship stress or family problems.**

☐ Strongly Disagree ☐ Disagree ☐ Neutral ☐ Agree ☐ Strongly Agree

## Total Comfort Score: ____ / 35

## CONTROL SMOKER STATEMENTS

● **I smoke most often when facing high-pressure situations or important decisions.**

☐ Strongly Disagree ☐ Disagree ☐ Neutral ☐ Agree ☐ Strongly Agree

● **Cigarettes help me think more clearly and focus my mind.**

☐ Strongly Disagree ☐ Disagree ☐ Neutral ☐ Agree ☐ Strongly Agree

● **I often smoke before or during stressful work situations.**

☐ Strongly Disagree ☐ Disagree ☐ Neutral ☐ Agree ☐ Strongly Agree

● **I started smoking during a time of high stress or major change.**

☐ Strongly Disagree ☐ Disagree ☐ Neutral ☐ Agree ☐ Strongly Agree

● **I use cigarettes to manage anxiety and worry.**

☐ Strongly Disagree ☐ Disagree ☐ Neutral ☐ Agree ☐ Strongly Agree

● **I have difficulty tolerating uncertainty.**

☐ Strongly Disagree ☐ Disagree ☐ Neutral ☐ Agree ☐ Strongly Agree

● **I smoke more when dealing with work pressure or perfectionist tendencies.**

☐ Strongly Disagree ☐ Disagree ☐ Neutral ☐ Agree ☐ Strongly Agree

## Total Control Score: ____ / 35

# PERFORMANCE SMOKER STATEMENTS

● **Cigarettes help me feel more confident and socially comfortable.**

☐ Strongly Disagree ☐ Disagree ☐ Neutral ☐ Agree ☐ Strongly Agree

● **I smoke most often in social or professional situations.**

☐ Strongly Disagree ☐ Disagree ☐ Neutral ☐ Agree ☐ Strongly Agree

● **I smoke more when under performance pressure.**

☐ Strongly Disagree ☐ Disagree ☐ Neutral ☐ Agree ☐ Strongly Agree

● **I use cigarettes to manage social anxiety or imposter syndrome.**

☐ Strongly Disagree ☐ Disagree ☐ Neutral ☐ Agree ☐ Strongly Agree

● **I started smoking to fit in with a group or image.**

☐ Strongly Disagree ☐ Disagree ☐ Neutral ☐ Agree ☐ Strongly Agree

● **I often smoke when working on creative projects or before presentations.**

☐ Strongly Disagree  ☐ Disagree  ☐ Neutral  ☐ Agree  ☐ Strongly Agree

● **I struggle to be authentic when I feel I'm being evaluated.**

☐ Strongly Disagree  ☐ Disagree  ☐ Neutral  ☐ Agree  ☐ Strongly Agree

## Total Performance Score: ____ / 35

## SCORING GUIDE

- **25-35 points**: This is your primary smoking personality.
- **15-24 points**: Secondary traits—these may influence you under stress.
- **Below 15**: Not a significant driver for you.

Remember, many people are mixed types. Your highest score points to your main pattern, but your healing journey may involve addressing elements of more than one.

## WHAT THIS MEANS FOR YOUR QUIT STRATEGY

Your smoking personality determines which Mind Map panels you're most likely to get stuck in, and which tools will help you most.

- **Comfort Smokers** often struggle with **Panels 1-2.** Healing requires learning to seek and accept support.
- **Control Smokers** often get stuck in **Panels 4-5.** Healing comes from tolerating uncertainty and developing inner stability.
- **Performance Smokers** often wrestle with **Panels 3** and **7.** Healing means separating worh from achievement and cultivating authentic confidence.

Understanding your personality is not about labeling yourself. It's about designing a quit plan that fits your psychology instead of fighting against it.

## CLOSING: BRIDGE TO CHAPTER 4

By now you should have a clear sense of your smoking personality. You may recognize yourself strongly in one type, or you may see parts of yourself in two or even all three. Either way, you've gained valuable insight into why cigarettes feel so compelling to you.

This understanding is the foundation for your personalized quit strategy. In the next chapter, we'll dig into what cigarettes are really providing for you psychologically and how to replace them with something real.

You'll see that what you thought was relief is actually an illusion. And once you see that clearly, quitting no longer feels like losing something. It feels like gaining your freedom back.

# CHAPTER 4.

## THE HOLE IN THE SOUL

### Understanding What Smoking Really Fills

# THE HIDDEN VOID

By now you've seen that smoking isn't really about nicotine. It's about something deeper, a need that was never fully met and a wound that never fully healed. In my practice, I call this the **hole in the soul**.

Every smoker I've ever treated carries this inner emptiness in some form. It isn't always dramatic trauma. Sometimes it's subtle—an emotional need overlooked, a feeling dismissed, a sense of being invisible. Other times it's the chaos of addiction in the family, an unpredictable home environment, or the pressure of conditional love.

Children are born whole—wired for connection, safety, and love. But when those needs aren't consistently met, something inside goes missing. It's not that the child is broken. It's that their natural wholeness was interrupted. The result is an emotional void that often follows them into adulthood.

This isn't about blaming parents. Most caregivers did the best they could with the tools they had. But the reality is, many people grew up with gaps in emotional attunement, and those gaps left them searching for comfort elsewhere.

That gap—that hunger for comfort, stability, or validation—is the hole in the soul.

# HOW THE HOLE IS CREATED

The hole in the soul forms when a child encounters one of these patterns:

- **Neglect or emotional unavailability**: A parent who provides physically but is absent emotionally or a parent who is both physically absent and emotionally unavailable.
- **Smothering or overcontrol**: A parent who doesn't allow independence, leaving the child unsure of their own identity.
- **Conditional love**: Care and approval that only come when the child performs or behaves a certain way.
- **Chaos or unpredictability**: An unstable environment shaped by addiction, conflict, or inconsistency.
- **Narcissistic parenting**: A parent's needs always taking center stage, leaving the child unseen.

Children can't step back and analyze, "My parent is struggling." They interpret unmet needs as

"I'm not important" or "I have to take care of myself." These beliefs become encoded deep inside and shape how they cope with life.

# HOW CIGARETTES FILL THE HOLE

When someone with a hole in the soul discovers cigarettes, it feels like magic. The cigarette becomes the missing piece. It provides the comfort, clarity, or confidence they never had.

- **Comfort Smokers** use cigarettes like a surrogate parent. They soothe loneliness and stress with a ritual that mimics comfort.
- **Control Smokers** see cigarettes as their focus tool, their way to create order and stay calm when life feels unsafe.
- **Performance Smokers** lean on cigarettes as a prop, a way to project confidence, appear creative, or fit in socially.

The first cigarette often feels like the solution the child never found. As one patient put it, "It was the first time I felt I could breathe."

But the relief is temporary. Cigarettes don't actually fill the hole. They only cover it, reinforcing the illusion that you need them to survive.

# JENNIFER'S HOLE IN THE SOUL

Jennifer, the nurse you met earlier, described smoking as her five minutes of "me time." To her, cigarettes felt like a way to be seen, a way to remind herself she existed.

But in truth, her smoking was born out of emotional invisibility. As a child, her parents were kind but emotionally distant. They didn't know how to engage with her feelings. Over time, she believed: "My emotions don't matter."

At sixteen, when she lit her first cigarette, it felt like something finally comforted her. But the comfort was false. Instead of teaching her to express her emotions and seek support, the cigarettes kept her quiet and alone.

By the time she became a mother, the illusion had unraveled. She wasn't more visible. She was more isolated. The cigarettes that promised comfort only deepened her loneliness.

# DAVID'S ILLUSION OF CONTROL

David, the financial advisor, grew up in a chaotic household with an unpredictable alcoholic father. As a boy, he learned to scan for danger, stay quiet, and control whatever he could.

When he found cigarettes in college, they felt like his anchor. "Lighting up made me think clearer," he said. "It was like flipping a switch to get back in control."

But as an adult, he noticed something unsettling. He was spending more mental energy managing his smoking—timing breaks, hiding the smell, worrying about running out—than managing his work.

The tool that was supposed to give him control had taken control. Cigarettes weren't calming him. They were ruling him.

## SHOSHANNAH'S FALSE CONFIDENCE

Shoshannah, the marketing creative, smoked mainly in social and professional settings. For her, cigarettes were a prop used to project sophistication and confidence.

She had grown up with conditional approval, where achievement meant love. By the time she reached her career, cigarettes felt like the accessory that completed her professional image. As she furthered her career, she abandoned her cigarette habit for vaping. This was "healthier" and "less gross." She felt like she had overcome her cigarette addiction.

But Shoshannah eventually admitted, "I felt like a fraud. I thought "quitting" cigarettes gave me confidence and security, but I've realized how only transitioning my habit to something that felt healthier was covering up how insecure al was really feeling about myself."

When she stopped relying on nicotine—either cigarettes or her vape—and began practicing authentic confidence, she discovered her creativity actually improved. The nicotine wasn't her muse. It was her mask.

## THE TRUTH

Comfort, control, and performance. Three powerful illusions. All of them fueled by the same emptiness.

Cigarettes don't heal the hole in the soul. They only pretend to. The comfort fades, the control crumbles, the performance collapses. And the hole is still there, waiting to be healed in healthier ways.

# THE GREAT DECEPTION

One of the most powerful illusions about smoking is that it calms you down. Nearly every patient I've treated has told me, "Cigarettes relax me. They help me cope with stress."

But here's the truth: cigarettes don't relax you. They stimulate you. Nicotine is a stimulant drug, which means it actually raises heart rate, increases blood pressure, and activates the nervous system.

So why do smokers feel calmer after lighting up? This is the *great deception*. What's really happening is relief from withdrawal. Your body, anxious for its next dose of nicotine, creates tension and unease. The moment you smoke, that tension briefly lifts. This is not because the cigarette relaxes you, but because it stops the withdrawal it caused in the first place. Nicotine is like the thief who robs your house, then shows up as the hero when he hands back your wallet.

# THE OXYGEN PARADOX

When you take that deep inhale of smoke, your lungs fill, your shoulders drop, and you exhale slowly. That's the moment you feel calmer. But the calm doesn't come from nicotine. It comes from oxygen and breath.

Your body has always known how to calm itself. Deep breathing activates the parasympathetic nervous system—the body's natural relaxation switch. Every time you inhale deeply and exhale slowly, your nervous system shifts toward calm.

The cigarette hijacks this process. It makes you believe the relief comes from nicotine when, in fact, the relief comes from your own breath. That's the *oxygen paradox*: you give the cigarette credit for the calm that was always yours.

Once you see this clearly, the cigarette loses much of its power. You realize you don't need it to breathe. That's why techniques like the 4-7-8 breathwork are so effective. They reclaim the very rhythm you once tied to smoking and return it in a purer, more powerful form.

# THE DOUBLE DUNGEON OF DARKNESS

The cigarette's deception doesn't end with the oxygen paradox. It also creates what I call the *Double Dungeon of Darkness*.

The first dungeon is the chemical addiction. Nicotine hooks into your brain's reward system, creating withdrawal symptoms when it's absent. You crave a cigarette to stop the discomfort.

The second dungeon is the psychological dependence. This is the belief that life without cigarettes would be unbearable. Smokers often say, "I won't be able to handle stress, or focus, or feel confident without them."

Together, these two dungeons form a trap. You feel locked in by both body and mind.

But here's the hopeful truth: neither door is really locked.

The chemical addiction fades within days once nicotine is out of your system. The psychological dependence collapses as soon as you recognize the illusions for what they are.

When you realize the cigarette was never your comfort, never your control, never your confidence, you see the bars of the dungeon for what they are: an illusion.

## THE HARSHEST COST: CANCER RISK

We can't talk honestly about smoking without mentioning cancer. Smoking is the leading cause of lung cancer, and it raises the risk of cancers of the throat, mouth, bladder, kidney, pancreas, and more. It also drives other devastating conditions—emphysema, heart disease, stroke, and even pregnancy complications such as "small-for-date" infants who enter the world already at a disadvantage. And it doesn't just harm the smoker. Side stream smoke exposes everyone around you to the same toxic chemicals, putting family, friends, children, and your pets at risk. Nicotine itself is a vasoconstrictor, meaning it tightens blood vessels, reduces circulation, and starves your organs—and your baby, if you're pregnant—of vital oxygen.

This isn't new information. From the bold warnings on cigarette packs to the commercials on TV, the world has made sure you know the dangers by heart. So much so that it can start to feel like the boy who cried wolf, repeated one too many times.

But fear of cancer and disease rarely creates lasting change. In my clinical experience, people don't quit for long because they're afraid. They quit for good when they connect with something more powerful: love for their family, pride in their health, or the freedom of living authentically.

So yes, the risk is real. But the lasting motivation will come from your *why*.

# WHAT THIS MEANS FOR YOU

Understanding the cigarette's deception is a turning point. When you see that:

- The calm was always from your breath, not from nicotine.
- The chemical and psychological prisons are illusions that can be unlocked.
- The health risks are real but fear alone isn't enough.
- You begin to take your power back.

Cigarettes never held the key. You did.

# SUCKING DOWN YOUR FEELINGS

Another way cigarettes deceive is by convincing you they help you avoid pain. Many of my patients have told me, "When I smoke, I don't feel as sad, angry, or stressed."

The truth is, smoking doesn't resolve those feelings. It suppresses them. Instead of experiencing sadness, you inhale smoke. Instead of facing anger, you exhale nicotine. Instead of allowing yourself to grieve, you light another cigarette.

I call this sucking down your feelings.

- **Comfort Smokers** suck down loneliness or rejection, burying the ache with smoke.
- **Control Smokers** suck down anxiety, hiding their worry behind the ritual of lighting up.
- **Performance Smokers** suck down insecurity, using cigarettes to mask self-doubt in social or professional situations.

In every case, the feelings don't disappear. They go underground, waiting. And the hole in the soul stays unhealed.

# THE CRACKED LENS OF PERCEPTION

When we carry childhood wounds, they act like a cracked lens over our eyes. We don't see reality clearly.

- Through the cracked lens, cigarettes look like friends instead of enemies.
- They look like comfort instead of poison.
- They look like control instead of dependence.
- They look like confidence instead of insecurity.

This distorted perception keeps smokers trapped. You believe you're choosing relief, when in reality, you're choosing chains.

Healing clears the lens. You begin to see cigarettes for what they really are: toxic sticks paper.

# PRACTICAL ALTERNATIVES

If cigarettes have been filling the hole in your soul, you'll need healthy replacements. Healing isn't just about stopping smoking, but instead about learning new ways to meet your emotional needs.

### For Comfort Smokers:

- **Support list**: Write down three people you can call when you feel lonely. Reach out instead of reaching for a cigarette.
- **Self-soothing rituals**: Replace smoke breaks with breathing through a straw, coffee stirrer or cinnamon stick,, herbal tea, exercise, or gentle breathing, or journaling.
- **Compassion mantra**: Try saying, "This is hard, and I deserve care."

### For Control Smokers:

- **4-7-8 breathwork**: Inhale for 4, hold for 7, exhale for 8. Repeat three times.
- **Uncertainty practice**: Let the dishes sit in the sink for an hour. Try a new route to work. Teach yourself to tolerate the unpredictable.
- **Reframing thoughts**: Instead of "If this goes wrong, it's a disaster," try "I've handled challenges before. I can handle this too."

### For Performance Smokers:

- **Values check-in**: Before a presentation or event, remind yourself of who you are beyond performance.
- **Authenticity practice**: Let yourself be genuine, even imperfect, in low-stakes situations. Notice that people respond to your real self.
- **Develop authentic confidence**: Try public speaking classes, creative classes (acting, improv, stand-up comedy), or physical training. These settings give you a safe place to stumble, recover, and try again as you grow skills that generate true self-belief.

These practices may seem small, but they directly target the illusions cigarettes have been sustaining. When failure is cushioned, you learn that facing challenges—not dodging them—is what builds real confidence. Each small win becomes part of a larger pattern, stacking into durable self-belief. With each practice, you discover that the strength you were chasing in a cigarette has been inside you all along.

# CHAPTER 5.

## BREAKING THROUGH YOUR DEFENSE MECHANISMS

### How to Dismantle the Barriers That Keep You Stuck

> **We erect defenses not to deceive others, but to deceive ourselves.** – Sigmund Freud

# WHY WE DEFEND WHAT HURTS US

The cigarette is not your friend. It's a crutch. It's a mask. It's a trick that keeps you small.

Psychologist Abraham Maslow taught that you can't reach self-actualization—the best version of yourself—until your basic needs are met. Smoking interferes with that. It numbs your feelings, blocks your growth, and convinces you that mere survival is the best you can hope for.

I call this the **Big "I"** versus the **little "i"**. The Big "I" is your self-actualized self: strong, authentic, fully alive. The little "i" is the reduced self: small, hidden, stuck. Cigarettes keep you in the little "i". They shut down your emotions so you don't confront your pain. And when you don't face pain, you don't grow. Smoking puts a lid on your psychological development, trapping you in a smaller version of yourself.

Defenses are the locks on that lid. They're like psychological bodyguards protecting you from painful truths but also protecting the cigarette's power over you.

And here's the thing: your defenses didn't come out of nowhere. They formed in childhood, when you didn't yet have the tools to face pain directly. Back then, minimizing, denying, or rationalizing may have helped you survive. They weren't weaknesses. They were strengths. But what once protected you is now the very thing keeping you stuck in the little "i".

Think about the last time someone questioned your smoking. Maybe you said, "*I only smoke when I'm stressed*," or "*I don't smoke that much*," or even, "*I could quit anytime I want*." Those are defenses at work. They sound reasonable. They shield you from shame. But they also keep you trapped.

In this chapter, we'll explore the most common defenses I see in smokers, how they operate, and—most importantly—how to break through them. Because every time you dismantle a defense, you take one step closer to the Big "I", the version of yourself cigarettes have been holding back all along.

# THE FIVE CORE DEFENSES IN SMOKERS

In my work, I see five defenses over and over again. Each one has its own voice, its own logic, and its own trap. Let's walk through them together:

### 1. Rationalization

**Definition**: Justifying your smoking with explanations that sound reasonable.

**Smoker's voice:**

- "I only smoke when I'm stressed."
- "Everyone needs something to take the edge off."
- "It helps me concentrate at work."

**Why it sounds true**: Because in the moment, smoking does feel like it helps. Stress fades temporarily, focus sharpens briefly. But as you learned in Chapter 4, that relief comes from oxygen and ritual, not nicotine.

**The trap**: Rationalization gives cigarettes credit they don't deserve. It allows you to keep smoking while telling yourself it's logical.

**Breaking through:**

- Identify the real source of relief. Was it the nicotine? Or was it the deep breath and pause?
- Challenge the logic. If smoking really helped stress, why does anxiety increase between cigarettes?
- Reframe. Try saying: "I don't need to explain smoking anymore. I need to understand what it's really doing to me."

## 2. Minimization

**Definition**: Downplaying the seriousness of your smoking.

**Smoker's voice:**

- "I don't smoke that much."
- "It's just a few cigarettes a day."
- "At least I'm not as bad as other smokers."

**Why it sounds true**: Because in comparison, your habit might look small. If your coworker smokes two packs a day and you smoke five cigarettes, it feels like "not much."

**The trap**: Minimization ignores the reality that even a few cigarettes a day harm your body, your mind, and your identity. It also keeps you from seeing how much mental energy from planning, hiding, and excusing your smoking still takes.

**Breaking through:**

- Drop comparisons. Your healing is about you, not about who smokes more or less.
- Count honestly. Write down every cigarette you smoke in a day. Numbers don't lie.

- Reframe. Instead of, "It's not that bad," try, "If it doesn't matter that much, then it should be easy to let it go."

# 3. Isolation

**Definition**: Separating your smoking from the rest of your life so you can avoid facing its impact.

**Smoker's voice**:

- "I never smoke around my kids, so it's fine."
- "I only smoke outside. It doesn't affect anyone else."
- "It's just my private thing."

**Why it sounds true**: Because it gives the impression you've contained the problem. By keeping smoking separate from work, family, or friends, you feel like you're controlling it.

**The trap**: Isolation hides the truth. Even if you never smoke in front of loved ones, they still see the effects in your smell, your cough, your absence during "smoke breaks." More importantly, it keeps you emotionally isolated. You carry your struggle alone instead of letting others support you.

**Breaking through**:

- Name the separation. Ask yourself: "Where in my life am I keeping smoking secret?"
- See the impact. Imagine how your child, partner, or friend feels when you disappear for a cigarette.
- Reframe. Instead of, "It's my private thing," try, "The more I hide this, the more power it has over me."

# 4. Denial

**Definition:** Refusing to acknowledge the seriousness of your smoking or your loss of control.

**Smoker's voice**:

- "I can quit anytime I want."
- "I'm not really addicted. I just like smoking."
- "It's not a big deal."

**Why it sounds true**: Because denial offers temporary relief from shame. If you tell yourself it's not a problem, you don't have to face the fear of change.

**The trap**: Denial delays healing. It keeps you stuck in the Double Dungeon of Darkness, convincing yourself the door is locked when it isn't.

**Breaking through:**

- Test the belief. If you could quit anytime, why haven't you?
- Acknowledge the pattern. Notice how many times you've told yourself "not a big deal" right before lighting up.
- Reframe. Instead of, "I can quit anytime," say, "I'm ready to prove to myself that I can quit now."

## 5. Projection

**Definition:** Shifting the blame for smoking onto others.

**Smoker's voice:**

- "Work stress makes me smoke."
- "If my partner didn't nag me, I wouldn't need cigarettes."
- "My friends smoke, so I can't quit around them."

**Why it sounds true:** Because stress, conflict, and social pressure do trigger cravings. It feels natural to blame outside forces.

**The trap:** Projection gives away your power. As long as smoking feels like someone else's fault, you can't take responsibility for change.

**Breaking through:**

- Own your choices: Stress and friends may be triggers, but only you decide to smoke.
- Reframe triggers: See them as opportunities to practice new coping strategies.
- Reclaim power: Say, "I can't control other people, but I can control my response."

# CASE STUDY: SARAH'S DEFENSES

You first met Sarah in Chapter 1. On the surface, she was a successful executive and devoted mother. Underneath, she was battling her defenses.

When her teenage daughter called her a hypocrite—"You tell me not to smoke, but you do it every day"—Sarah's defenses began to crumble.

- **Rationalization:** "I'm under too much stress at work. This is the only way I can cope."
- **Minimization:** "I don't smoke as much as I used to. It's not that bad."
- **Isolation:** "I only smoke outside. My family doesn't even notice."
- **Denial:** "I could stop tomorrow if I wanted. I'm just not ready."
- **Projection:** "If my boss didn't put so much pressure on me, I wouldn't need cigarettes."

Each defense bought her a little more time. But each one also deepened her shame and exhaustion.

The breakthrough came in a moment of honesty. After her daughter's confrontation, Sarah sat down and wrote in her journal: "If I could quit tomorrow, I already would have. The truth is, cigarettes are controlling me. And I hate that."

That single admission cracked the armor. The defenses collapsed, and the real healing could begin.

## REFLECTION

Do you recognize yourself in any of these defenses? Maybe you've said you only smoke outside, or that stress makes you do it, or that you can quit whenever you choose.

Notice the defenses without judgment. What once protected you now keeps you stuck. Awareness is the first step in breaking through.

Every time you see a defense clearly, you loosen its grip. Through that opening, your authentic self can step forward.

## CASE STUDY: MEGAN'S STORY

Megan is 24 now, but the wound she carries started in childhood. Her father was a stand-up comedian, the kind of dad who could light up a room with laughter and made her feel adored. But he also lit up something else.

At every family party, he'd slip outside for a smoke. During every outing, there was a stop at the store because he needed another pack. Megan loved her dad and he loved her, but the cigarettes always seemed to come first. The message she absorbed—even if he never meant it that way—was that nicotine mattered more than time with her.

Today, Megan doesn't smoke. She never has. But her father's habit still lingers in her life in unexpected ways. When she dates, she gets intensely triggered if she discovers someone smokes, vapes, or hides any compulsive habit. It doesn't even have to be nicotine. What sets her off is the secrecy—the feeling that something else will always take priority over her.

For Megan, her father's smoking wasn't just about his health. It became a template for how love can feel conditional, divided, or overshadowed by addiction. The weight of that memory sits on her shoulders even now, shaping her search for trust and safety in relationships.

Her story is a powerful reminder: smoking doesn't just affect the smoker. It weaves into the lives of children, partners, and loved ones in ways that last long after the smoke clears. If you can't yet find a reason to quit for yourself, let Megan's story be a mirror. Do it for the small one who looks up to you, who loves you more than anything, and who deserves your presence more than your cigarettes. That is a real *why*.

# THE CHOICE POINT: BREAKDOWN OR BREAKTHROUGH

Every smoker eventually reaches a crossroads. The defenses that once worked begin to fail. Rationalizations sound hollow. Minimizations feel dishonest. Denial collapses under reality.

This is what the Mind Map calls **Panel 6: Breakdown or Breakthrough**.

At this stage, you face two options:

- **Breakdown**: Reinforce your defenses and sink deeper into chaos. You convince yourself to smoke more in secret, minimize harder, or push away those who confront you.
- **Breakthrough**: Allow the defenses to crack. Admit the truth. Feel the vulnerability. Face the hole in the soul instead of covering it.

Breakthrough takes courage. It feels like stepping into the unknown without armor. But it's also the beginning of real freedom.

One of my patients once said, "When I finally admitted I wasn't in control, I thought I was falling apart. But that was actually the beginning of me coming together."

# A CLINICAL METHOD FOR BREAKING DEFENSES

So how do you move from breakdown to breakthrough? Here's the process I use with patients. It's simple but powerful:

1. **Identify your defense.** Notice which excuse you use most often. Is it rationalization? Minimization? Denial?
2. **Understand its purpose.** Remember: your defense once protected you. It kept you safe as a child when you couldn't face the full weight of your pain.
3. **Recognize how it traps you now.** Ask yourself: how is this defense keeping me stuck as a smoker?
4. **Choose vulnerability.** Instead of hiding behind the excuse, tell yourself the truth. Admit the craving. Admit the struggle. Say it out loud or write it down.
5. **Take a small action step.** Do something that contradicts the defense. If you say, "I don't smoke that much," write down every cigarette you smoke in a day. If you say, "I smoke because of stress," try 4-7-8 breathing instead. If you say, "It's private," tell someone you trust that you're struggling.

Breaking defenses isn't about tearing yourself down. It's about telling yourself the truth and building strength on honesty instead of illusion.

# WARNING SIGNS THAT DEFENSES ARE AT WORK

You'll know your defenses are active if you notice yourself saying or thinking things like:

- "It's not that bad."
- "I'll quit later."
- "I only smoke in certain situations."
- "I'm not like heavy smokers."
- "I'm under too much stress right now."
- "People are making me smoke."

These phrases may sound harmless, but they're red flags. They're signals that your defenses are trying to keep you from facing the truth. The moment you catch one of these thoughts, pause. Don't attack yourself. Simply notice: "Ah, that's my defense talking." Awareness is the crack in the armor.

# THE FREEDOM IN HONESTY

When Sarah finally admitted, "Cigarettes are controlling me," she felt exposed and ashamed. But within weeks, she told me it was the most freeing sentence she'd ever written.

Honesty feels risky at first, but it creates space for transformation. Defenses keep you locked in fear. Truth opens the door to healing.

*Remember*: every time you challenge a defense, you strengthen your authentic self. Each crack in the armor is progress. Each moment of honesty is victory.

# CLOSING: PREPARING FOR CHAPTER 6

Defenses are natural. They are part of being human. But they don't have to run your life anymore. You can thank them for the protection they once gave you, and then let them go.

Now that you've seen through the illusions and begun breaking your defenses, it's time to face another challenge: the false positive associations that cigarettes still hold in your mind. These are the beliefs that make cigarettes seem like friends instead of enemies.

In the next chapter, we'll dismantle those positive associations through a powerful technique called *aversion therapy*. It's the method that turns cigarettes from comfort into disgust, from companion into repulsion. It's the next step in breaking the nicotine spell for good.

# CHAPTER 6.

## AVERSION THERAPY

### Breaking The Positive Associations With Cigarettes

- Unknown

# THE BREAKUP YOU NEED TO HAVE

You can't quit smoking if you still secretly believe cigarettes are your friend. That's the single biggest obstacle I see in my patients.

Even after recognizing the hole in the soul (Chapter 4) and breaking through defenses (Chapter 5), many smokers still cling to the idea that cigarettes help them. They convince themselves that smoking brings relief, focus, or confidence.

The reality is you can't break up with cigarettes if you still think you're in love with them.

This is where aversion therapy comes in. Aversion therapy is a method designed to strip away the false romance. It replaces the positive associations you've built around cigarettes with negative ones. It forces you to see smoking clearly, not as comfort or control, but as the poison it really is.

# THE NARCISSISTIC RELATIONSHIP WITH CIGARETTES

Think of cigarettes like a narcissistic partner—one that pretends to care for you but really takes more than it gives.

At first, cigarettes love-bombed you. They made you feel rebellious, grown-up, or sophisticated. They promised relief and identity.

Then they began gaslighting you. They told you they were relaxing you, even though nicotine was making your body more anxious. They whispered, "You can't cope without me," even as you were always the one providing calm through your own breath.

Over time, cigarettes began to control you. They dictated when you could take breaks, how you spent your money, even who you spent time with. They pulled you away from loved ones at dinner, outside at parties, or into isolation at work.

Finally, came the devaluation. What once felt like comfort now left you coughing, ashamed, and worried about your health. You wanted to stop, but the cigarette kept saying, "You'll never leave me. You need me."

# REFRAMING THE RELATIONSHIP

This isn't about shaming you. It's about calling cigarettes out for what they really are. They're liars. They're manipulators. They promise comfort and leave you feeling alone. They promise control and keep you dependent. They promise confidence and leave you insecure.

Once you see that, you stop defending cigarettes. You stop buying the story. You don't need their fake charm anymore.

That's where **aversion therapy** comes in. It's the tool that makes this undeniable. It flips the script. Cigarettes go from "my friend" to "my enemy." From something you reach for to something you want nothing to do with.

# WHAT AVERSION THERAPY IS

Aversion therapy is a structured exercise that helps you detach emotionally from cigarettes. It works by confronting the cigarette directly, noticing its reality, and creating a powerful negative association.

Instead of seeing smoking as soothing, you begin to see it as revolting. Instead of associating it with relief, you associate it with harm. Instead of craving it, you want nothing to do with it.

The process may sound uncomfortable, but discomfort here is progress. It's not punishment, it's truth-telling. Aversion therapy makes the unconscious belief that cigarettes are "helpful" collapse under the weight of reality.

# WHY IT WORKS

Cigarettes have had decades of good press in your brain. They've been linked to comfort, focus, confidence, rebellion, or relaxation. But these links are illusions. Aversion therapy works by rewiring those connections.

Neuroscientists have a phrase for it: *what wires together, fires together*. Every time you lit up and felt relief, your brain locked the two together. Cigarette equals comfort. That's conditioning.

Aversion therapy flips the script. When you repeatedly pair cigarettes with honest, negative experiences—the harsh taste, the smell, the mirror reflection—you recondition your brain. Now smoking equals disgust, not desire. That's the point we want to get to. A point I affectionately call **Destination Disgust**.

And once that shift happens, the cigarette loses its power.

# CARLA'S STORY

Carla, a 36-year-old patient, described her smoking as "being stuck in a toxic relationship."

"When things got stressful, I'd run to cigarettes the way someone runs back to a bad partner," she said. "They gave me a few minutes of comfort, but left me feeling worse afterward, whispering, *'Without me, you're nothing. You can't handle life on your own.'* And part of me believed it. And every time I did, I felt smaller."

Carla's turning point came during aversion therapy. Standing in front of the mirror, she watched herself inhale. She noticed the harsh lines of smoke clouding her face, the tightness around her eyes, the stale smell clinging to her hair. "It hit me," she told me. "This isn't love. This is abuse. I don't need it anymore."

From that moment, Carla's perspective changed. She no longer saw the cigarette as a source of comfort. She saw it for what it was: a manipulator she was finally ready to leave.

When Carla finally walked away from her "toxic boyfriend," the change didn't happen overnight. At first, she admitted she still heard the voice. *"Come back. You need me."* But this time, instead of obeying, she laughed at it. "It felt like hearing from an ex who still thought he had power over me," she said. "Only now, I could see right through him."

Aversion therapy had given her the break she needed. Each time she looked in the mirror, she no longer saw a savior but a manipulator. And once that illusion broke, the cigarette's grip was gone. "For the first time in years," Carla told me, "I felt like I was in control of the relationship, not him. I finally chose me."

# RECLAIMING YOUR POWER

When you finally see smoking for the toxic, one-sided relationship that it is, everything changes. Cigarettes never cared about you. They never gave you comfort, control, or confidence. Like a vampire, they sucked you dry—of your health, your money, your energy—and left you weaker every single time.

Aversion therapy makes that truth impossible to ignore. It rips away the fake charm and shows you what's really there: poison, dependence, and control. The illusion of comfort dies the second you see what it's really doing to you.

And here's the moment that matters most: when you decide, *"I don't need this bloodsucker in my life anymore,"* the spell breaks. The cigarette stops feeding on you. And you finally get your power back.

# THE AVERSION THERAPY PROTOCOL

Aversion therapy is the foundation of this program. Whether you choose the **cold turkey** method or **gradual withdrawal**, you'll begin here. This protocol lays the groundwork by breaking nicotine's false charm and rewiring your brain before you quit for good.

Aversion therapy applies to all nicotine products—cigarettes, e-cigarettes, vape pens, and nicotine pouches. The form may differ, but the trap is the same.

- **With vapes**: Notice the chemical taste, the sticky residue in your mouth, the way the device clings to your hand. Write down the cost, the smell, and how often you find yourself reaching for it.
- **With nicotine pouches**: Notice the bitterness, the numbness in your gums, the hassle of keeping them stocked, and the quiet shame of hiding them.

Whether cigarette, vape, or pouch, the principle is the same: stop romanticizing. Start associating the product with what it really is: poison, dependence, and control. The steps you're about to learn can be applied to any nicotine product you use.

The following steps form the protocol I use with patients. Whether you're taking the **cold turkey approach**, or you're using the **gradual withdrawal approach**, aversion therapy is what you'll practice daily until your quit date. Each session only takes 5–10 minutes, but the effect builds quickly.

## Step 1: Prepare Your Environment

- Choose a time and place where you won't be interrupted.
- Remove cigarettes from convenient spots; keep them in one inconvenient location.
- Gather the following:
- A mirror (for visual confrontation).
- Cinnamon sticks, coffee stirrers, or straws (for clean breathing practice).
- A journal for recording your reflections.
- A glass jar with a little water on the bottom.

### Step 2: Retrieve a Cigarette

- Take one or two cigarettes from the inconvenient spot.
- Notice the effort it took just to get them.

### Step 3: Mirror Confrontation

- Stand or sit in front of the mirror.
- Look into your eyes as you hold the cigarette.
- Notice your skin, your teeth, your expression.
- Remind yourself: "This cigarette has harmed me. It does not deserve a place in my life."

**SAFETY ALERT**

**\*IF YOU EXPERIENCE DIZZINESS, LIGHTHEADEDNESS, SHORTNESS OF BREATH, CHEST PAIN, OR ANY OTHER CONCERNING SYMPTOMS, DISCONTINUE IMMEDIATELY AND SEEK GUIDANCE FROM A QUALIFIED MEDICAL PROFESSIONAL BEFORE CONTINUING.**

### Step 4: Mindful Inhalation

- Light the cigarette slowly and deliberately.
- Take one or two deep puffs and cough it up.
- Instead of numbing out, pay close attention to the harshness of the smoke, the bitterness of the taste, the irritation in your throat or lungs.
- Blow smoke into a tissue or handkerchief. Notice the discoloration it leaves behind.

### Step 5: Immediate Replacement

- Put the cigarette down in an ashtray or somewhere safe.
- Pick up your cinnamon stick, coffee stirrer, or straw.
- Take three to five deep breaths through it, filling your lungs with clean air.
- Notice the contrast: the fresh oxygen soothes you while the cigarette harms you.

### Step 6: Repeat the Cycle

- Go back to Steps 4 and 5 and complete them two more times.
- When finished with your aversion session, extinguish the cigarette in your jar of water.

- Place each used cigarette in the jar of water. At the end of every session, take a brief sniff to reinforce just how foul and disgusting cigarettes really are. Return to the jar any time you need a quick reminder.

### Step 7: Journal Reflection

- Write down exactly what you experienced.
- Be honest about the taste, the smell, and the feelings.
- Reinforce the truth: *"Cigarettes are not my comfort. They are my poison."*

### Step 8: Repeat Daily

- **Cold Turkey approach**: Practice aversion therapy every time you smoke during your five-day stop-smoking plan.
- **Gradual Withdrawal approach**: Practice aversion therapy once a day for 3 weeks or less. Your last cigarette before you quit for good will be done aversion style.

Repetition is what makes aversion therapy effective. Each session builds disgust, rewires your associations, and weakens the cigarette's hold.

# SAMPLE SELF-TALK

During your aversion sessions, I encourage you to use truth statements like:

- "I see you for what you are, not what I thought you were."
- "You don't comfort me—you harm me."
- "I'm done letting you lie to me."
- "I choose clean air over poison."
- Speaking the truth out loud makes the break more powerful.

# TAILORING AVERSION THERAPY BY PERSONALITY

Every smoker experiences aversion therapy a little differently. To make it as effective as possible, adapt the exercise to your smoking personality.

### Comfort Smokers

- As you smoke, reflect on how the cigarette deepens your loneliness rather than relieving it.
- Journal about times you smoked to avoid asking for support.

- Replace the cigarette with a self-soothing ritual: calling a friend, making tea, writing down one kind thing you'll do for yourself.

### Control Smokers

- As you smoke, notice how much energy you spend planning, hiding, or worrying about smoking.
- Reflect on how cigarettes actually add to your anxiety.
- Replace the cigarette with a calming practice like the 4-7-8 breathwork.

### Performance Smokers

- As you smoke, confront the illusion that cigarettes give you confidence or creativity.
- Journal about times you felt strong or inspired without smoking.
- Replace the cigarette with a ritual that builds authentic confidence: a power pose, a grounding breath, or jotting down three strengths you bring to the moment.

## WHY TAILORING MATTERS

Aversion therapy is not a one-size-fits-all exercise. The more you connect it to your personal smoking pattern, the faster the illusions collapse. Each time you pair smoking with truth and disgust, you weaken the false bond. Each time you replace it with a healthier ritual, you strengthen your new identity.

## SIGNS THAT AVERSION THERAPY IS WORKING

- How will you know if the process is taking hold? Watch for these signs:
- Cigarettes or vapes start to smell worse than before.
- Your first puff feels disgusting instead of calming.
- You notice yourself craving clean air more than nicotine.
- The urge to smoke fades faster than it used to.
- You catch yourself thinking, "I don't even want this."

These are milestones. They may seem small, but they signal a massive shift that the illusions are breaking.

## CASE STUDY: MARCUS'S TURNING POINT

Marcus, the ER nurse you met earlier, resisted aversion therapy at first. "Why would I make myself smoke like this on purpose?" he asked.

But when he finally tried it, the shift was dramatic. Standing in front of the mirror, he lit a cigarette slowly. Instead of rushing through, he noticed every detail: the bitter taste, the acrid smell, the way his shoulders tightened instead of relaxing.

After one puff, he put it out. "It tasted like chemicals. I felt stupid holding it. I looked in the mirror and thought, This is what my patients see when I tell them not to smoke? I never want to see myself like that again."

Within days, Marcus reported that cigarettes tasted worse. By the end of the week, he felt more disgust than desire. "It was like my brain flipped a switch," he said. "I stopped craving the lie."

## ENCOURAGEMENT AND REFRAMING

Aversion therapy can feel uncomfortable. That's the point. It strips away the illusions you've built around smoking. It takes away the romance and forces you to see the cigarette for what it is: a manipulative, narcissistic partner that never cared about you.

But remember, discomfort here is not failure. It's growth. Every time you feel disgust instead of craving, you are reclaiming your freedom.

When you notice a cigarette smells foul, celebrate it. When your first puff makes you cough instead of calm, celebrate it. When you put one out after a single drag because you don't even want it, celebrate it.

These are not setbacks. They are signs that you're healing.

## CLOSING: PREPARING FOR CHAPTER 7

You're about to dismantle one of the cigarette's last strongholds—the false positive associations. You will experience the truth: cigarettes never gave you comfort, control, or confidence. They lied to you, just like a toxic partner does.

Aversion therapy helps you see those lies clearly. It makes the cigarette disgusting instead of desirable. It flips the script so quitting feels like empowerment, not deprivation.

In the next chapter, we'll build on the power of aversion therapy. You'll choose your path—cold turkey or gradual withdrawal—and design a personalized quit plan based on your smoking personality. This is where the rubber meets the road. It's where the transformation you've been preparing for begins to take lasting form.

7.

# CHAPTER

## CHOOSING YOUR PATH

### Building Your Personalized Quit Plan

> " A goal without a plan is just a wish.
> –Antoine de Saint-Exupéry "

# THE POWER OF CHOICE

Up to this point, you've exposed the hole in the soul and learned how to dismantle your defenses and break the false romance with cigarettes. You're beginning to see the truth: smoking never gave you comfort, control, or confidence. It just made you think that.

Now comes the moment that separates insight from action.

You've got to decide how you're going to quit.

There are two paths: **Cold Turkey** or **Gradual Withdrawal**. Both work. I've used both in my practice for decades. The right one is the one that fits you.

Picture yourself at a crossroads. Both roads lead to freedom. The only difference is which one you're ready to take. Your choice. Your pace. Your power.

# THE COLD TURKEY APPROACH

**Definition**: Cold Turkey means quitting completely on a chosen quit date. No tapering, no cutting back. You stop smoking and start living smoke-free immediately.

For many people, this is the most direct path to freedom. Once nicotine is out of your system, your body begins healing within hours. Withdrawal symptoms typically peak within two to three days and then start easing. By the end of the first week, most of the physical cravings are gone.

**Strengths of Cold Turkey**:

- Fastest route to detox.
- Simple—no schedules, no gradual reduction to track.
- Creates a clean break, which some personalities find empowering.
- Forces you to immediately build new coping skills.

**Challenges of Cold Turkey**:

- Can feel intense in the first 48–72 hours.
- Requires emotional readiness and tolerance of discomfort.
- May trigger relapse if attempted without preparation.

**Best For**:

- People with strong motivation and a compelling *"why."*
- Smokers who dislike dragging things out.

- Those who respond well to "all or nothing" decisions.
- Performance Smokers who benefit from bold, dramatic action.

## CASE STUDY: DANIEL'S COLD TURKEY QUIT

Daniel, a 52-year-old teacher, had smoked for more than thirty years. "I tried to taper down a dozen times," he told me. "But every time I cut back, I found ways to sneak in more."

Daniel chose a cold turkey quit date that coincided with the start of summer break. He prepared by cleaning his house, throwing out every ashtray and lighter, and telling his colleagues and family about his plan.

The first three days were difficult. He described feeling restless, irritable, and distracted. The aversion therapy exercises were helping him break the positive associations with smoking. He used the 4-7-8 breathing technique every time cravings hit, sometimes repeating it ten times a day. By Day 5, his energy lifted. By Week 2, he realized he could walk up stairs without gasping. By Week 4, he said, "I feel like I've gotten years of my life back."

For Daniel, cold turkey worked because he was emotionally ready and fully committed.

## THE GRADUAL WITHDRAWAL APPROACH

Definition: Gradual Withdrawal means cutting back systematically for two to three weeks before the final quit date. Instead of stopping suddenly, you eliminate cigarettes in categories or blocks, reducing your intake step by step until you quit completely.

For many patients, this approach eases anxiety. It gives them practice with cravings, teaches them to use new coping skills, and helps them feel less overwhelmed.

**Strengths of Gradual Withdrawal:**

- Gentler transition.
- Builds confidence by showing you can manage without certain cigarettes.
- Allows time to integrate new coping tools before the final quit.
- Works well for Comfort Smokers who fear losing their "soothing" time.

**Challenges of Gradual Withdrawal:**

- Requires structure and discipline to avoid dragging it out.
- May prolong cravings if not followed consistently.
- Can tempt you to rationalize more—"I'll just cut back longer."

**Best For**:

- Smokers who feel anxious about quitting suddenly.
- People with unpredictable or high-stress schedules.
- Those who respond well to gradual change and small wins.
- Control Smokers who prefer order and structure.

# CASE STUDY: MARISOL'S GRADUAL WITHDRAWAL

Marisol, a 41-year-old mother of two, described cigarettes as her "tiny escapes." She lit up in the car on the way to work, after meals, and during stressful evenings. "The thought of giving them all up at once felt impossible," she admitted.

So we built a gradual plan together. In Week 1, she eliminated her morning cigarette, replacing it with a five-minute journaling ritual. In Week 2, she cut her after-lunch cigarette, taking a ten-minute walk instead. By Week 3, she was down to her "identity cigarettes"—the evening ritual she thought she couldn't live without.

Those were the hardest to let go, but she leaned on her sister for support and used the **Hee-Hee breathing technique** whenever cravings hit. (This is a simple exercise: inhale deeply through your nose, then exhale sharply in short bursts—*hee, hee, hee*—as if you're pushing the craving out of your body.) Each time she did it, the urge lost its grip.

By her quit date, Marisol was already living most of her day smoke-free. And when she finally cut the last cigarette, she told me, "It felt like closing the final chapter of a bad story."

Gradual Withdrawal worked for Marisol because it gave her the space to build confidence step by step. Each small win stacked into the strength she needed to quit for good.

# THE DECISION MATRIX

So which path is right for you—Cold Turkey or Gradual Withdrawal? The answer depends on your personality, your circumstances, and your readiness.

Here are some questions to guide your choice:

- Do I handle discomfort well, or do I panic quickly?
- Do I prefer fast results, or does gradual change feel more manageable?
- What's my current stress level?
- Do I have strong support around me right now?

· Do I tend to be "all or nothing," or do I thrive with step-by-step progress?

Choose Cold Turkey if...

· You're highly motivated by your "why."
· You dislike dragging things out.
· You've had success before with bold, decisive changes.
· You're prepared for a few tough days up front.

Choose Gradual Withdrawal if...

· Quitting all at once feels overwhelming.
· You want to practice new coping tools before your final quit date.
· You thrive with structure and incremental progress.
· Your life circumstances (stress, family, health) make a gentler approach easier.

Remember, there is no wrong choice. Both paths lead to freedom. The best path is the one that feels sustainable to you.

**MEDICAL DISCLAIMER**

*This program and the strategies described in this book are for educational purposes only. They are not intended to replace professional medical advice, diagnosis, or treatment. Nicotine is a powerful drug, and quitting can affect both your physical and mental health.*

*Always consult your physician or another qualified healthcare provider before beginning any smoking cessation program, especially if you have chronic medical conditions (such as heart disease, diabetes, COPD, or high blood pressure), are pregnant or breastfeeding, or are taking prescription medications.*

*Do not disregard professional medical advice or delay seeking it because of something you read in this book.*

*If you experience severe withdrawal symptoms, chest pain, dizziness, shortness of breath, or any other concerning medical issues, stop the program immediately and seek medical attention.*

*Your health and safety come first. Use this program as a supportive framework, but work in partnership with your healthcare team for the best outcome.*

Dr. Judy Rosenberg

# Final Preparation
## Checklist Items

No matter which method you choose, preparation is key. The more thoroughly you prepare, the higher your chances of success. Use this checklist to get ready:

☐ **Medical Considerations:** If you have chronic health conditions, consult your doctor before quitting. Ask about medication adjustments if you're on treatments impacted by nicotine.

☐ **Environmental Prep:**

- Keep away from alcohol and any other substances that can impair your judgement or will-power.
- Remove cigarettes, vapes, lighters, and ashtrays from your home and car.
- Wash clothes, clean upholstery, and deep clean your space to remove smoke smell.
- Replace smoking cues with positive ones (candles, plants, fresh air).

☐ **Nutritional Support:**

- Stock up on healthy snacks (fruits, nuts, vegetables) to manage hand-to-mouth cravings.
- Stay hydrated. Water helps flush nicotine and reduces withdrawal symptoms.
- Support your brain and body with targeted supplements (more detail below).

☐ **Support System Activation:**

- Choose at least one accountability partner you can text or call when cravings hit.
- Inform close family or friends of your quit date and ask for encouragement, not criticism.
- Consider joining a support group (in person or online).

☐ **Psychological Preparation:**

- Write your *"why"* on index cards or sticky notes and place them where you'll see them often (bathroom mirror, car, wallet).
- Visualize yourself living smoke-free—breathing easier, waking up refreshed, being more present with loved ones.
- Commit with a clear statement: *"I am ready. I will no longer let cigarettes control me."*

# NUTRITIONAL SUPPORT FOR QUITTING

Nicotine addiction isn't only psychological. It also affects your body chemistry. Smoking depletes key nutrients, increases oxidative stress, and disrupts mood regulation. Supporting your system nutritionally can make withdrawal smoother.

Here are the nutrients most important during the quit process:

- **Vitamin C** – Smoking rapidly depletes Vitamin C. Restoring it reduces oxidative stress and supports immunity.
- **B Vitamins (B6, B12, Folate)** – Critical for mood, energy, and nervous system balance. Quitting often increases demand.
- **Magnesium** – Helps calm the nervous system and ease cravings.
- **Vitamin D** – Supports mood stability; deficiency is common and worsens under stress.
- **Omega-3s (EPA/DHA)** – Promote brain health and reduce irritability.
- **Adaptogens (Rhodiola, Ashwagandha)** – Herbs that reduce stress reactivity and fatigue.

SUPPLEMENT DISCLAIMER

*THE NUTRITIONAL INFORMATION IN THIS SECTION IS FOR GENERAL EDUCATIONAL PURPOSES ONLY AND IS NOT A SUBSTITUTE FOR PROFESSIONAL MEDICAL ADVICE. ALWAYS CONSULT YOUR PHYSICIAN OR A LICENSED HEALTHCARE PROVIDER BEFORE STARTING ANY NEW SUPPLEMENT, VITAMIN, OR HERBAL REGIMEN—ESPECIALLY IF YOU ARE PREGNANT, BREASTFEEDING, HAVE CHRONIC HEALTH CONDITIONS, OR TAKE PRESCRIPTION MEDICATIONS.*

*INDIVIDUAL NEEDS VARY, AND SOME SUPPLEMENTS MAY INTERACT WITH MEDICATIONS OR MEDICAL CONDITIONS. RESEARCH HAS ALSO SHOWN THAT HIGH-DOSE BETA-CAROTENE SUPPLEMENTS MAY INCREASE LUNG CANCER RISK, PARTICULARLY IN SMOKERS. WHOLE-FOOD SOURCES SUCH AS CARROTS AND LEAFY GREENS REMAIN SAFE AND BENEFICIAL.*

*USE THIS INFORMATION AS A GUIDE FOR DISCUSSION WITH YOUR HEALTHCARE PROVIDER, NOT AS A PRESCRIPTION.*

# A FORMULA TO SUPPORT YOU

Quitting smoking isn't just about breaking the habit. It's also about helping your body recover. Many smokers are depleted in Vitamin C, B vitamins, magnesium, and Omega-3s, which play key roles in mood, energy, and resilience during withdrawal.

To make this process easier, I partnered with Reserve Labs to create a **clinical-grade supplement blend** designed specifically to support your body and brain through nicotine withdrawal. It combines these key nutrients into one formula, so instead of juggling multiple bottles, you can give your system the reinforcement it needs in a single step.

## * Learn more at kickitdrjudy.com

This is not a magic pill. But it can provide your body with a strong nutritional foundation to stabilize, recover, and adjust as you step into your new smoke-free life.

**\*IMPORTANT NOTE:** THIS SUPPLEMENT IS NOT INTENDED TO DIAGNOSE, TREAT, CURE, OR PREVENT ANY DISEASE. ALWAYS CONSULT YOUR PHYSICIAN BEFORE BEGINNING ANY NEW SUPPLEMENT PROGRAM, ESPECIALLY IF YOU ARE PREGNANT, BREASTFEEDING, MANAGING CHRONIC CONDITIONS, OR TAKING PRESCRIPTION MEDICATIONS.

# SUPPORT SYSTEM ACTIVATION

Quitting smoking is a personal journey, but it isn't one you need to walk alone. A strong support system can mean the difference between relapse and resilience.

The key is to ask for the kind of support you need, not the kind that adds guilt or pressure. Many of my patients tell me, "I don't want people to nag me or shame me." What they needed instead was encouragement, patience, and understanding.

## Here's how to build your support system:

1. Identify Your Team

- **Cheerleader:** someone who celebrates small victories with you.
- **Accountability Partner:** someone you can text or call when a craving feels overwhelming.
- **Safe Space Person:** someone who listens without judgment when emotions get heavy.

## 2. Set Clear Expectations

- When you tell your team about your quit date, be specific:
- "I may be irritable at first. Please be patient."
- "I need encouragement, not criticism."
- "If I relapse, don't shame me. Help me get back on track."

## 3. Lean on Support When Experiencing Triggers

- Call a friend instead of reaching for a cigarette.
- Text your accountability partner during cravings.
- Spend more time with non-smokers during your first weeks.

Support doesn't erase the challenge, but it amplifies your strength. When you know someone has your back, it's easier to stay committed.

# FINAL PSYCHOLOGICAL PREPARATION

Quitting smoking isn't just about removing cigarettes, it's about stepping into a new identity. To reinforce your commitment, I recommend three powerful practices.

## 1. Write and Sign a Quit Contract

On paper, write:

> "I commit to quitting smoking permanently. I will not let cigarettes control me any longer. I am choosing health, freedom, and authenticity."

Sign and date it. Place it somewhere visible. This isn't just a piece of paper, it's a declaration to yourself.

**\*To make it even easier, we've created a printable Quit Contract you can download at kickitdrjudy.com. Print it, sign it, and claim your commitment in writing.**

## 2. Visualization Exercise

- Close your eyes and picture yourself six months from now:
- Breathing freely as you walk up stairs.
- Smiling as your child hugs you without smelling smoke.
- Feeling confident in a meeting without needing a cigarette first.

Visualization isn't wishful thinking. It's training your brain to expect success.

Dr. Judy Rosenberg

### 3. Positive Reinforcement for Strength

**Repeat daily:**

- "I am ready."
- "My body is healing."
- "I am stronger than cigarettes."
- "I choose freedom."

Positive thinking may feel simple, but words shape beliefs. Speak them outloud. Every time you repeat them, you strengthen your new identity.

### 4. Protect Your Decision-Making

In the first weeks of quitting, steer clear of alcohol and anything else that messes with your judgment. One drink, one buzz, one moment of lowered guard—and cigarettes are right there waiting to pounce. Don't hand your power back over a glass of wine. Protect your clarity. Protect your choice.

# THE POWER OF FULL COMMITMENT

One truth I share with all patients: addiction loves ambiguity. If you leave even a small back door—"Maybe I'll smoke at parties" or "I'll just keep one pack around"—cigarettes will find a way back in.

Commitment closes the door. Not because you'll never struggle, but because you won't negotiate with the addiction anymore. You've made your choice.

# CLOSING: PREPARING FOR CHAPTER 8

It is now time to make your program choice—**Cold Turkey** or **Gradual Withdrawal**. You've set yourself up with medical awareness, a clean environment, nutritional support, a team in your corner, and the right mindset.

That's your foundation. And preparation is power.

Next, we move into action. **Chapter 8** walks you through the **Gradual Withdrawal** program step by step.

If you've already decided **Cold Turkey** is your path, you can **skip ahead to Chapter 9** and jump straight into the plan.

Either way, this is the line in the sand. Insight is over. Action starts now. Look to the next page— your freedom begins here.

# CHAPTER 8.

## THE 3-WEEK GRADUAL WITHDRAWAL PROGRAM

### Your Day-by-Day Roadmap to Freedom

> **Great things are not done by impulse, but by a series of small things brought together.** –Vincent Van Gogh

# THE PROMISE

You've thought about quitting. You've talked about it. You've told yourself, *"One day, I'll finally kick this thing."*

Well, this is that day.

This is where you stop circling the idea and start breaking the chains. And those chains? They're not a metaphor you can ignore. Look at the cover of this book. Those shattered links represent the prison you've been living in. Nicotine forged every one, puff by puff, day after day. Every time you lit up, you welded another bar onto your own cage.

The plan you're about to follow isn't about cutting back for comfort. It's about smashing those links, one by one, until nothing is left but broken chains.

Here's the promise: by the end of this chapter, you'll know exactly what to do each day, why you're doing it, and how it leads you to freedom. No confusion. No gray areas. You'll wake up knowing, *"This is today's step. This is how I break another link in the chain."*

Let's be clear about this: gradual withdrawal isn't permission to stall. It's a training program—mental, physical, and emotional—that prepares you for your clean break. Think of it as strength conditioning for the final fight. That final moment when you *KICK IT* for good.

**\*If you're a vape user,** this protocol applies to you just as much as it does to cigarette smokers. The device may look different, and the flavors may disguise it, but the psychology is the same. Nicotine cravings, withdrawal symptoms, and emotional triggers don't change whether you smoke or vape. When I say "cigarette" in this chapter, know that the same steps apply to your vape.

Building a habit takes roughly 3 weeks of conistency. Breaking a habit takes more than subtraction; it takes a mindset shift. This 21-day plan does both. You'll still smoke or vape briefly while retraining your brain, but each replacement, each craving resisted, each aversion practiced rewires you for freedom.

Here's what's ahead:

- **Week 1:** Awareness & Easy Wins
- **Week 2:** Substitution & Confidence
- **Week 3:** Retiring the Identity Cigarettes and Saying Goodbye Forever

Follow it exactly, and by Day 21 you'll feel the weight of those chains fall away.

# WHY GRADUAL WITHDRAWAL WORKS

Not everyone feels ready to quit all at once. For many smokers, the thought of giving up every cigarette on the same day feels overwhelming. That doesn't mean you're weak. It means your psychology needs a different approach.

Gradual withdrawal works by dismantling the habit piece by piece. Instead of asking you to give up everything overnight, it guides you to eliminate cigarettes in stages. Each week, you'll reduce specific "categories" of smoking while practicing new coping skills. By the end of three weeks, the cigarettes that once felt essential no longer fit your life.

This method is particularly effective for:

- **Comfort Smokers** who fear losing their "soothing" moments.
- **Control Smokers** who prefer structure and order.
- **Performance Smokers** who need to practice authentic confidence before giving up cigarettes in social or high-pressure settings.

Gradual withdrawal is not about dragging your feet. It's about building confidence through small wins. Every day you follow the plan, you weaken the cigarette's grip and strengthen your freedom.

# RULES OF THE GAME

Before we start, let's set the rules. These aren't "try-ifs." They're the foundation. Follow them and succeed; bend them and stay chained.

### Rule 1:
### NO CIGARETTES OR VAPE HITS OUTSIDE THE PLAN

If a cigarette is marked for removal, it's gone. Not "maybe tomorrow." Gone. The only smokes that exist are the ones this plan tells you to take.

### Rule 2:
### REPLACE EVERY PUFF WITH SOMETHING BETTER

The craving isn't only for nicotine, it's also for ritual. So every time you cut a puff, *insert* a new one: a cinnamon stick, straw, sugar-free gum, herbal tea, or better yet—*oxygen*.

## Rule 3:
### JOURNAL DAILY

Every cigarette you cut has a story. Log time, emotion, situation, and defense mechanism. Awareness kills autopilot.

## Rule 4:
### USE YOUR BREATHING TOOLS

Your two weapons: *4-7-8 breathing* to calm your nervous system, and *Hee-Hee breathing* to push urges out. Oxygen is the real medicine.

## Rule 5:
### TALK BACK TO THE URGE

DOWNLOAD WORKBOOK
AT KICKITDRJUDY.COM

Craving shows up? Answer it *out loud*.

- "My body wants oxygen, not nicotine."
- "This isn't comfort; it's a chain. I'm breaking it now."
- "Health begets health. I choose health. Every time."

## Rule 6:
### FUEL YOUR RECOVERY

Nicotine drains vitamins and dehydrates you. Replenish: hydrate, move daily, eat real food, supplement wisely. Every healthy act is another crack in the chain.

Memorize these. Post them. Because tomorrow you start Week 1, and that's when the real work begins.

# ADAPTING THE PLAN TO YOUR SMOKING PERSONALITY

The Five-Day Aversion Plan works for all smokers, but tailoring it to your smoking personality makes it even more effective.

### COMFORT SMOKERS:

- Focus on how cigarettes deepen your loneliness instead of relieving it.
- During mirror confrontation, remind yourself: "This cigarette does not comfort me. It isolates me."
- Journal about times when smoking made you feel invisible or disconnected.
- Replace the after-session craving with real comfort: a phone call, a hug, or journaling.

## CONTROL SMOKERS:

· Focus on how cigarettes add to your anxiety instead of reducing it.
· During mindful inhalation, say: "This cigarette doesn't calm me. It makes me more nervous."
· Journal about how much energy you spend managing your smoking (hiding, planning, worrying).
· Replace cravings with box breathing or short, structured breaks that restore calm.

## PERFORMANCE SMOKERS:

· Focus on how cigarettes undermine your confidence instead of boosting it.
· During mirror confrontation, remind yourself: "This cigarette doesn't make me look confident. It makes me look dependent."
· Journal about times you performed well or connected socially without smoking.
· Replace cravings with confidence-building rituals: power poses, affirmations, or values check-ins.

# MINDSET PREVIEW — THE 21-DAY FRAME

Before you dive into the day-by-day work, lock this in your head: breaking a habit isn't just about stopping. It's about re-coding your identity. So as you start Week 1, remember:

· You're not "cutting down." You're training for freedom.
· Each skipped puff is a vote for your future.
· Every day you repeat a new behavior, you're teaching your brain who's in charge.

At the end of the 21 days, we'll revisit this mindset and lock it in for good. For now, keep this truth in view:

**"Breaking the habit starts with action, but it lasts because of mindset."**

You know the *why*. Now it's time to start the work.

**\*If you're a *VAPE USER*, this protocol applies to you just as much as it does to cigarette smokers. The device may look different, and the flavors may disguise it, but the psychology is the same. Nicotine cravings, withdrawal symptoms, and emotional triggers don't change whether you smoke or vape. When I say "cigarette" in this chapter, know that the same steps apply to your vape.**

# WEEK 1 – AWARENESS & EASY WINS

**GOAL:** Track every smoke or vape session, identify your weakest links throughout the day, remove them one at a time (or in multiples if you have a heavy habit), and practice replacing each one with healthier rituals.

This is the week you loosen the first chains.

## How This Week Works

You're not quitting yet, you're learning your enemy. Awareness is the first crack in addiction's armor.

For seven days, your job is to watch yourself like a scientist: when, where, and why you light up. By the end of the week, you'll have already cut the weakest link cigarettes or vape sessions and proven that you—not nicotine—decide what happens next.

> *Remember: **every skipped puff replaced with oxygen is a hammer blow to the chain. Small actions repeated daily create the break.***

## DAY 1

☐ **TRACK EVERY CIGARETTE OR VAPE HIT TODAY.**
Write the time, emotion, and situation for each.
Example: "8:15 a.m.—stressed, before meeting."

*No judgment.* **Just data.**

☐ **MARK WHICH ONES FELT WEAKEST.**

The automatic smokes you barely notice are your first targets. Star them in your journal.

**SCRIPT FOR TODAY:** "I can't break what I can't see. Awareness breaks autopilot."

## DAY 2

☐ **KEEP TRACKING EVERY PUFF.**

- Log time, emotion, and trigger.
- Notice patterns: Boredom? Stress? Habit?

☐ **CHOOSE YOUR WEAKEST LINK CIGARETTES OR VAPE HITS.**

Write them down: _____

_____

**JOURNAL PROMPT:** "What emotion or situation sparks these the most?"

## DAY 3

☐ **REMOVE YOUR MORNING WEAKEST LINK CIGARETTES OR VAPE HITS.**

- Often the early-morning or mid-morning one. It's gone.
- Don't "make it up later."

☐ **REPLACE IT IMMEDIATELY.**

- Drink a tall glass of water.
- Step outside for sunlight.
- Do three rounds of 4-7-8 breathing.

☐ **LOG THE EXPERIENCE.**

"Skipped my 9:30 smoke. Breathed instead. Restless → calm in 3 min."

**SCRIPT FOR TODAY:** "My body wants oxygen, not nicotine."

## DAY 4

☐ **REMOVE YOUR MID-DAY WEAKEST LINK CIGARETTES OR VAPE SESSIONS.**

☐ **REPLACE THEM.**

- Five-minute walk.
- Hee-Hee breathing.
- Piece of fruit or handful of nuts.

☐ **KEEP YOUR REPLACEMENT TOOLS VISIBLE.**

Cinnamon stick, straw, gum, or herbal tea—anything to fill the ritual gap.

**JOURNAL PROMPT:** "Which excuse hit hardest today and how did I answer it?"

## DAY 5

☐ **REMOVE YOUR EVENING WEAKEST LINK CIGARETTES OR VAPE SESSIONS.**

☐ **REPLACE THEM.**

- Hot cup of tea.
- Hot bath.
- Stretching, yoga, meditation.

☐ **KEEP YOUR REPLACEMENT TOOLS VISIBLE.**

Cinnamon stick, straw, gum, or herbal tea. Make sure it's within arm's reach.

**SCRIPT FOR TODAY:** "Comfort isn't in nicotine; it's in action."

## DAY 6

☐ **STAY CONSISTENT.**

- Continue skipping all removed cigarettes or vape hits.
- Keep using replacements until they feel automatic.

☐ **OBSERVE CHANGES.**

Notice the shifts in your energy, focus, mood, or breathing.

**JOURNAL PROMPT:** "What feels easier or clearer now that these cigarettes are gone?"

## DAY 7

☐ **REVIEW YOUR WEEK.**

- Flip through your notes.
- Circle repeated triggers and emotions.

☐ **REFLECT.**

Write one or two truths that surprised you.

Example: "I wasn't craving nicotine, I was craving quiet."

☐ **STRENGTHEN YOUR NEW RITUALS.**

Keep the morning, afternoon, and evening replacements solid.

**SCRIPT FOR TODAY:** "I'm already weakening the chains. I can feel the bonds breaking."

## END OF WEEK 1 REFLECTION

You've removed your daily weakest link cigarettes or vape sessions, built awareness, and proven you can act differently. That's more than small progress, it's the first fracture in the addiction's armor.

**Write this affirmation in your journal:**

*"I'm not waiting to be free. I'm already taking my freedom back, one link at a time."*

## WEEK 2 - SUBSTITUTION & CONFIDENCE

**GOAL:** Replace your routine cigarette/vape hits—after I wake up, after I eat, after I finish work, etc.—with healthier rituals while practicing daily aversion training. By the end of this week, you'll be swinging the hammer hard enough to shatter your toughest chains.

## YOUR DAILY AVERSION APPOINTMENT

Starting this week, you'll use aversion, your most powerful tool.

**HERE'S THE RULE:** you'll do one aversion session every day at the same time. This is not random or optional. It's an appointment. Treat it like showing up for work or therapy. It matters that much. Same time, every day. Non-negotiable.

MY AVERSION APPOINTMENT TIME: _____

Set a daily alarm, write it on your calendar, and commit. Consistency is what rewires your brain.

## AVERSION TRAINING: STEP-BY-STEP

At your scheduled time, do the following:

- **Go to your cigarettes that you've stashed in your chosen inconvenient location.** Don't make it easy to access. The friction is part of the training.
- **Stand in front of a mirror.** Look yourself in the eyes.
- **Light a cigarette or take a vape hit.** Take one or two mindful puffs only. Do this at least three rounds per session.
- **Notice what's real**: the taste, the smell, the burn, the cough.
- **Switch immediately to 4-7-8 breathing.** Oxygen—not nicotine—is what your body craves.
- **Drop the butt or pod into a glass of water.** Watch it hiss and drown. That sound is the chain breaking.
- **Journal one line**: "Clean air feels better than this."

Repeat this every day. Your goal is to reach what we call **Destination Disgust**.

That's the point where your brain finally says, "I'm done." Sometimes it takes three rounds, sometimes it takes more. Remember, the goal is to reach your "Destination".

**SAFETY NOTE:** If you feel dizzy or nauseated, STOP IMMEDIATELY. If you're high-risk (cardiac or respiratory issues, pregnancy), use the gentle version: look, smell, and taste awareness only—no deep inhalation.

## HOW THIS WEEK WORKS

This is where you turn awareness into control. You'll replace the cigarettes you used to "earn" or "reward" yourself with better rituals. Each one will reinforce your power, not your prison.

These routine smokes (after breakfast, after work, after dinner) are what we call "chain links of comfort." This week, you'll prove comfort doesn't come from nicotine, it comes from choice.

## DAY 8

☐ **SCHEDULED AVERSION SESSION (AT CHOSEN TIME)**

> Follow the 7-step process. Repeat until you hit **Destination Disgust**.

☐ **REPLACE THE AFTER-BREAKFAST CIGARETTE.**

- Brush your teeth right after eating.
- Brew herbal tea.
- Step outside for **2 minutes of 4-7-8 breathing.**

☐ **SCRIPT FOR TODAY**: "Nicotine never made breakfast better. Oxygen does."

## DAY 9

☐ **SCHEDULED AVERSION SESSION**

> Same time, same steps. Disgust takes repetition.

☐ **REPEAT YOUR AFTER-BREAKFAST RITUAL.**

- Teeth → tea → breathing.
- Focus on how clean it feels to start your day without smoke.

☐ **JOURNAL PROMPT**: "What lie did I believe about my morning cigarette—and what truth replaces it?"

## DAY 10

☐ **SCHEDULED AVERSION SESSION**

☐ **REPLACE YOUR MID-DAY CIGARETTES.**

- Take a 5-minute walk.
- Do one round of 4-7-8 breathing.
- Hydrate with a tall glass of water.

☐ **SCRIPT FOR TODAY**: "My body doesn't need nicotine. It needs movement."

## DAY 11

☐ **SCHEDULED AVERSION SESSION**

☐ **REPEAT THE MID-DAY REPLACEMENT RITUAL.**

- Walk → 4-7-8 breathing → water.
- Take note: you're alert and calm—something nicotine never truly gave you.

☐ **JOURNAL PROMPT:** "How did the walk feel compared to a cigarette break?"

# DAY 12

☐ **SCHEDULED AVERSION SESSION**

☐ **REPLACE THE AFTER-DINNER CIGARETTE.**

- Brew tea or herbal drink.
- Write three lines about your day.
- Stretch or take a short walk.

☐ **SCRIPT FOR TODAY:** "This isn't a nightcap. It's a chain. I'm breaking it now."

# DAY 13

☐ **SCHEDULED AVERSION SESSION**

☐ **REPEAT YOUR AFTER-DINNER REPLACEMENT.**

- Tea → journaling → stretch/walk.
- Focus on calm, not craving.

☐ **JOURNAL PROMPT:** "What did I gain tonight by not smoking?"

# DAY 14

☐ **SCHEDULED AVERSION SESSION**

☐ **REVIEW YOUR WEEK'S REPLACEMENTS.**

- Morning: tea + oxygen ritual.
- Afternoon: walk + water.
- Evening: tea + journal + stretch.

☐ **REFLECTION EXERCISE.**

- Write the moments you felt genuine disgust toward smoking this week.
- Name one "chain link" you've broken permanently.

☐ **SCRIPT FOR TODAY:** "I'm not reducing. I'm recovering. Every day I'm breaking chains."

## END OF WEEK 2 REFLECTION

By Day 14, your "routine" cigarettes are gone, replaced with rituals that actually restore you. You've also logged seven straight days of aversion. That's seven deliberate hammers to the chainlinks of illusion.

Look back at your journal. Circle words like disgust, control, relief, peace.

That's the new story you're writing.

Write this declaration: *"I'm not losing cigarettes. I'm smashing chains. I'm recovering the truth that nicotine always tried to hide."*

# WEEK 3 – RETIRING IDENTITY CIGARETTES

**GOAL:** Eliminate your "signature" cigarettes—the ones tied to your personality—and close out the 3-week plan with a decisive goodbye that seals disgust and freedom into your mind forever.

By the end of this week, your physical habit will be fading, your emotional triggers will have weakened, and your new identity will have taken root. This is the week where you prove: you're not trying to quit, you already have.

If that sentence feels too bold right now, good. Growth should feel a little impossible before it becomes real.

## DAILY CHECKLIST STRUCTURE

You're still keeping your Scheduled Aversion Session at the same time every day. This rhythm matters. It reinforces control and consistency, two things nicotine never gave you.

**MY AVERSION APPOINTMENT TIME:** _____

Every day starts with your aversion hammer, then moves into targeting one of your "identity cigarettes." These are the final locks on the door of your physical and psychological prison.

## DAY 15

☐ **SCHEDULED AVERSION SESSION (AT CHOSEN TIME)**

- Go to your inconvenient stash location.
- Mirror + 1–2 mindful puffs → cough → 4-7-8 breathing.
- Drop butt/pod into water jar.

☐ **JOURNAL:** "Clean air feels better than this."

☐ **TARGET CIGARETTE: THE EVENING RITUAL**

- Skip your usual after-dinner smoke.
- Take a warm shower instead.
- Put on music, a podcast, or read.
- Call or text a growth partner for accountability.
- End with 3 rounds of 4-7-8 breathing.

☐ **SCRIPT FOR TODAY:** "I don't need poison to end my day. I need peace."

# DAY 16

☐ **SCHEDULED AVERSION SESSION**

- Follow the same process.
- Focus on reaching Destination Disgust.

☐ **REPEAT YOUR NEW EVENING RITUAL.**

Replace nicotine with calm, connection, and oxygen.

☐ **JOURNAL PROMPT:** "What does real peace feel like without nicotine?"

# DAY 17

☐ **SCHEDULED AVERSION SESSION**

Mirror → puff → disgust → jar → 4-7-8 → journal.

☐ **REINFORCE YOUR NEW EVENING RITUAL.**

Add something meaningful: light stretching, gratitude journaling, or quiet reflection.

☐ **SCRIPT FOR TODAY:** "I'm learning to relax the real way."

# DAY 18

☐ **SCHEDULED AVERSION SESSION**

☐ **TARGET CIGARETTE: THE SOCIAL SMOKE**

- Before going out, tell one ally: "I'm practicing new rituals tonight. No cigs/No vape."
- Step outside with smokers if you need to, but don't light up.

- Hold a drink, straw, or cinnamon stick for the hand habit.
- Focus on the truth: connection doesn't require combustion.

☐ **SCRIPT FOR TODAY:** "I don't need nicotine to belong. I belong because I'm me."

# DAY 19

☐ **SCHEDULED AVERSION SESSION**

☐ **REPEAT YOUR SOCIAL TEST.**

- Face another social setting without smoking.
- Notice how saying no feels more powerful than saying yes.

☐ **JOURNAL PROMPT:** "What surprised me about staying smoke-free around others?"

☐ **SCRIPT FOR TODAY:** "Real confidence doesn't come from a lighter. It comes from choice."

# DAY 20

☐ **SCHEDULED AVERSION SESSION**

☐ **TARGET CIGARETTE: THE CREATIVE/FOCUS SMOKE**

- Before starting work or a project, do 2 minutes of 4-7-8 breathing.
- After finishing, take a 3-minute walk or stretch.
- Observe: focus and creativity aren't enhanced by nicotine—they're liberated without it.

☐ **SCRIPT FOR TODAY:** "My creativity comes from me, not from smoke."

☐ **JOURNAL PROMPT:** "What did I accomplish today because I stayed smoke-free?"

# DAY 21 — THE FINAL GOODBYE

This is it—your last cigarette, your last puff, your last chain.

☐ **SCHEDULED AVERSION SESSION (FINAL SESSION)**

- Go to your inconvenient stash location.
- Stand in front of the mirror. Look yourself in the eyes.
- Light a cigarette or vape. Take 1 or 2 mindful puffs, or as many as it takes to get to Destination Disgust.
- Feel it: the burn, the taste, the cough, the shame.

- Say out loud: "Goodbye. You no longer control me."
- Drop it into the water jar. Watch it hiss, drown, and die.
- Destroy all remaining cigarettes or vape devices. Crush them. Toss them.
- Toss the jar. Or keep it as a reminder of your former disgusting habit.

☐ **JOURNAL THIS MOMENT.**

"This was my last cigarette. This was the last link. I am free."

☐ **SCRIPT FOR TODAY:** "I don't smoke. I KICKED IT."

## END OF WEEK 3 REFLECTION

You've completed 21 days. You've tracked, replaced, and demolished the illusion. You've felt disgust where you once felt comfort, and you've proven that nicotine has zero power left.

Open your journal and read it front to back. Those pages are your proof, a written record of your freedom being reclaimed.

Now write this declaration, loud and clear:

*"I'm not a smoker. I'm not a vaper. I'm free. I broke the chains."*

Then look at the cover of this book again. Those shattered links? That's you now.

## CLAIM YOUR KICK IT DIPLOMA

You did it. You reached Destination Disgust and broke your final chain. Now it's time to make it official.

Go to **KickItDrJudy.com/Diploma** and download your Kick It Diploma.

Choose the **Gradual Withdrawal Program Diploma.** Print it. Write your name in bold letters. Sign it. Date it. Frame it.

This isn't just a piece of paper. It's your certificate of victory—a visible reminder that you didn't just try to quit...you KICKED IT.

Every time you look at that diploma, you'll remember exactly the discipline, the disgust, and the decisions that it took to get here. It's your daily reminder that freedom isn't temporary, it's who you are now.

The 21-Day Plan built your freedom. In chapter 10, we'll ensure you secure it.

# THE THRESHOLD

Twenty-one days ago, you were trapped in the Double Dungeon—caught between the wound that created your habit and the defenses that kept you chained to it. You couldn't see the way out because the chains felt like safety.

Look at where you stand now.

You've systematically dismantled the illusion, link by link. You've replaced false comfort with real calm. You've learned that the oxygen your body craves was always the answer—not the nicotine that hijacked the ritual. You've proven, day after day, that you are stronger than the habit that once controlled you.

But here's what you may not fully realize yet: the physical habit is only half the story.

These 21 days weren't just about cutting cigarettes or vape hits. They were about cracking the code of your psychological operating system. Every time you said no to a craving, you were voting for your future self. Every time you chose breathing over burning, you were rewriting the story your brain had been telling itself for years.

That's called a paradigm shift. And whether you've fully felt it yet or not, it's already happening inside you.

## WHAT'S CHANGING INSIDE YOU

In my practice, I've watched this transformation unfold in thousands of patients. The gradual approach creates something powerful: a slow, steady erosion of the smoker identity and the simultaneous construction of something new.

You may have already noticed the signs:

- Moments where you forgot to think about smoking—not because you were fighting it, but because it simply wasn't on your mind.
- A flash of disgust when you smell smoke on someone else—and the realization that you used to smell exactly like that.
- A breath that feels deeper, cleaner, more satisfying than any puff ever did.
- A quiet voice inside you that says, "I don't do that anymore"—not as a struggle, but as a simple fact.

These aren't small changes. They're tectonic. They're the tremors that signal your identity is shifting at its foundation.

# FROM BREAKING CHAINS TO BUILDING FREEDOM

The 21-Day Plan was designed to do exactly what its name promised: break the chains. You've done that. The links are shattered. The cage door is open.

But freedom isn't just about escaping a prison. It's about learning to live in the light, and that requires a different kind of work.

In Chapter 10, we'll explore what happens when the paradigm shift takes hold. You'll learn to recognize the moment when cigarettes finally lose their spell over you. You'll understand how to build a new identity that isn't just "a smoker who quit," but someone for whom smoking no longer makes sense because it does not reflect who you are now.

This is the difference between white-knuckling through cravings for the rest of your life and living as someone who simply doesn't smoke.

# YOUR NEXT STEP

Before you turn the page, take a moment to acknowledge what you've accomplished.

Open your journal and write today's date. Then write this declaration:

*"I broke the chains. I've reached Destination Disgust. Now I'm ready to build my new life."*

Sign it. Mean it.

The hardest work is behind you. What's ahead isn't another battle, it's an acknowledgement that your new you is finally in control of creating better outcomes for your life.

Chapter 10 is where you'll learn to secure your freedom forever. Let's finish what you started.

**Note:** Because you completed the 21-Day Gradual Withdrawal Plan, skip Chapter 9 (which covers the Cold Turkey approach) and go directly to **Chapter 10: The Paradigm Shift** on **Page 117.** Your transformation continues there.

# CHAPTER 9.

## THE 5-DAY COLD TURKEY AVERSION PLAN

> **Great things are not done by impulse, but by a series of small things brought together.** –Vincent Van Gogh

# INTRODUCTION — THE BIG DECISION

You're not tapering. You're not easing out. You're cutting the chain clean.

If you're here, it means you've already made the hardest choice: to stop letting nicotine call the shots. You're ready to end this habit in five focused days. That's not a fantasy. It's a formula that works.

This plan is fast, structured, and intense. Think of it as a five-day boot camp for your brain. Each day, you'll run one aversion session at a set time, log what happens, and reinforce the truth: nicotine is not your comfort, it's your cage.

By the end of Day 5, most people can't even finish a puff. The smell, the taste, the idea of smoking becomes repulsive. That's what we call **Destination Disgust**—the moment your brain flips the switch from craving to rejection.

And yes, it's uncomfortable. It's supposed to be. That discomfort is your nervous system learning that oxygen is the real reward.

**Reality Check:**

The first 72 hours are where your body fights hardest. As nicotine leaves your system, expect cravings, irritability, fatigue, brain fog, and restlessness. This isn't punishment. It's your body and mind healing. Your nicotine level is dropping and your dopamine and serotonin levels are re-balancing. When the discomfort hits, remember that every craving is your brain resetting to normal, not breaking down. Breathe through it with the 4-7-8 or Hee Hee breathing technique.

The symptoms peak quickly and fade faster than it feels. You can do this. You know exactly what it takes.

# PREPARE FOR KICK IT DAY (BEFORE YOU BEGIN)

Preparation is power. You wouldn't walk into a championship fight without gear. Don't walk into this one unarmed.

## CHOOSE YOUR 5-DAY WINDOW

Pick five consecutive days when you can focus—a stretch with minimal stress, travel, or major events. Many people start on a Thursday so their toughest cravings hit over a weekend.

Mark all five days on your calendar. Circle the final one in bold and label it Kick It Day: My Last Cigarette.

## SET YOUR AVERSION APPOINTMENT TIME

Every day for the next five, you'll have one appointment with yourself. Same time. Same place. No negotiation.

Write it down here and treat it like a meeting you cannot miss:

**MY AVERSION APPOINTMENT TIME:** _____

Set a reminder on your phone. Post-it on your mirror. Consistency rewires the brain faster than motivation ever could.

## GATHER YOUR TOOLS

*To make this process as easy as possible, we've prepared a number of downloadable documents such as a follow along journal, Freedom Contract, and printable Aversion Session steps at **KickItDrJudy.com.**

- **Mirror:** For confronting the illusion. You need to see yourself smoking to break the fantasy.
- **Glass jar half-filled with water:** For aversion. Dropping the butt or pod into the jar makes the disgust visible and final.
- **Cinnamon stick or straw:** For oral replacement when urges strike outside the session.
- **Journal or Notebook:** To track each session, thoughts, and disgust level (1–10). Awareness kills autopilot.
- **Freedom Contract:** Your personal accountability pact—keep it where you can touch it daily.
- **Support Partner:** One person you'll text "DONE" after every session. Accountability keeps momentum alive.
- **Rapid Relief Toolkit:** Breathing card, mints, water, movement plan, hot tea—everything you'll need for cravings.
- **Fill your refrigerator with healthy foods.** You'll need to replace essential vitamins and minerals such as Vitamins C and B, magnesium, and Omega-3 Fatty Acids (See **Page 106** for more details).

## CREATE YOUR QUIT SPACE

Designate a small area—bathroom mirror, garage, balcony—where you'll do every aversion session.

Keep it uncluttered and consistent. When you step into that space, your brain will learn: *"This is where I end the habit."*

## TELL YOUR SUPPORT CIRCLE

Announce it. Tell a friend, partner, or coworker: "I'm going cold turkey for five days."

Saying it out loud makes it real. You've turned an idea into a public declaration.

## RATE YOUR STARTING POINT

Open your journal and write:

- **Craving Level: ___/10**
- **Confidence Level: ___/10**
- **Reason I'm Doing This/Your Big WHY:** _____

This is your baseline. You'll look back at these numbers on Day 5 and realize how far you've come.

## SET YOUR INTENTION

Before you close this prep section, write this sentence by hand:

"I am starting my 5-Day Kick It Plan on _____.

I will show up every day, keep my promise, and arrive at Destination Disgust."

Sign and date it. You just gave your future self a command.

## WHAT TO EXPECT PHYSICALLY

Within the first three days, you may notice headaches, dry mouth, coughing, changes in appetite, or light dizziness. These are classic signs that your body is detoxing. Stay hydrated, eat real food, and rest when you can. Don't let your energy levels drop. If you feel tense, use 4-7-8 breathing or Hee-Hee breathing to calm your nervous system. If you feel tired, that's okay—your body is redirecting energy to repair itself.

## KNOWING YOUR WHY

Intention is causal. Why are you doing this? Define your Big *"WHY."*

Before you dive into the daily work, *remember this*:

## Breaking a habit cold turkey isn't just about stopping; It's about re-coding your identity fast.

In the next five days, your brain will begin to reset its reward system—the circuitry that used to link nicotine with comfort or control.

Each aversion session in this program will strike directly at that wiring, replacing old associations with new ones: disgust, clarity, confidence, and freedom.

This is not a waiting game. It's a reprogramming sprint.

But before you begin, you need one thing that no plan can provide — your **Big *WHY***.

Your *WHY* is the emotional engine that drives you through discomfort.

It's what keeps you steady when cravings whisper, when old habits try to pull you back, and when your mind looks for loopholes.

Take a breath.

DOWNLOAD WORKBOOK
AT KICKITDRJUDY.COM

Now, ask yourself with total honesty:

- Why am I doing this?
- What moment, thought, or event finally pushed you to take your power back?
  - Was it your health?
  - Your family?
  - Your kids watching you?
  - The way you smell after smoking?
  - The way your body feels when you wake up?
  - The part of you that's tired of feeling controlled by something smaller than you?

Whatever it is — write it down. Be specific. Be raw.

**My Big *WHY***: _____

This is your reason. This is your *Cause*. Every time an urge surfaces, come back here and reread it.

Let your why remind you that you're not just quitting cigarettes—you're taking back authorship of your own life.

So as you start Day 1, remember:

- You're not "cutting down." You're cutting loose.
- Each puff you face and reject is a vote for your future.
- Every time you reach Destination Disgust, you're teaching your brain who's in charge.

By the end of these five days, your body will be detoxed, your cravings will fade, and your identity will shift from smoker to self-directed human being.

**Keep this truth in view:** "Breaking the habit starts with action, but it lasts because of mindset."

You've defined your intention, and intention is causal. Now you know your Big *WHY*. It's time to start the work.

# ADAPTING THE PLAN TO YOUR SMOKING PERSONALITY

The Five-Day Aversion Plan works for all smokers, but tailoring it to your smoking personality makes it even more effective.

## COMFORT SMOKERS:

- Focus on how cigarettes deepen your loneliness instead of relieving it.
- During mirror confrontation, remind yourself: "This cigarette does not comfort me. It isolates me."
- Journal about times when smoking made you feel invisible or disconnected.
- Replace the after-session craving with real comfort: a phone call, a hug, or journaling.

## CONTROL SMOKERS:

- Focus on how cigarettes add to your anxiety instead of reducing it.
- During mindful inhalation, say: "This cigarette doesn't calm me. It makes me more nervous."
- Journal about how much energy you spend managing your smoking (hiding, planning, worrying).
- Replace cravings with box breathing or short, structured breaks that restore calm.

## PERFORMANCE SMOKERS:

- Focus on how cigarettes undermine your confidence instead of boosting it.
- During mirror confrontation, remind yourself: "This cigarette doesn't make me look confident. It makes me look dependent."
- Journal about times you performed well or connected socially without smoking.
- Replace cravings with confidence-building rituals: power poses, affirmations, or values check-ins.

# NEXT STEP:

You're equipped. You have your tools, your time slot, your contract, and your *why*.

Next, you'll begin *DAY 1*. Follow each checklist exactly. No shortcuts. No "almosts." This is the start of your clean break, and the last time nicotine ever dictates a single move you make.

Once you have completed these steps, you are ready to begin. This process does not require anything complicated. It only takes onsistency, focus, and a willingness to follow the sequence exactly.

# THE DAY-BY-DAY EXPERIENCE

Every day of the Five-Day Plan has its own rhythm. Some days feel harder than others, but each one serves a purpose. Here is what to expect.

# DAY 1

## ☐ 1.YOUR FIRST AVERSION SESSION

- The first session may feel strange, even uncomfortable.
- You may notice resistance: "Why am I doing this? This feels awkward."
- This is normal. Awareness itself is progress.

*I will list the steps for the Aversion Session you will perform each day of this program. Please use it for Day 1 and refer back to it for Days 2 through 5. You can also download and print the steps for the Aversion Sessions from KickItDrJudy.com/Aversion.

### AVERSION SESSION STEPS:

### Step 1: Prepare Your Environment

- Choose a time and place where you won't be interrupted.
- Remove cigarettes from convenient spots; keep them in one inconvenient location.
- Gather the following:
  - A mirror (for visual confrontation).

- Cinnamon sticks, coffee stirrers, or straws (for clean breathing practice).
- A journal for recording your reflections.
- A glass jar with a little water on the bottom.

## Step 2: Retrieve a Cigarette

- Take one or two cigarettes from the inconvenient spot.
- Notice the effort it took just to get them.

## Step 3: Mirror Confrontation

- Stand or sit in front of the mirror.
- Look into your eyes as you hold the cigarette.
- Notice your skin, your teeth, your expression.
- Remind yourself: "This cigarette has harmed me. It does not deserve a place in my life."

**SAFETY ALERT**

**\*IF YOU EXPERIENCE DIZZINESS, LIGHTHEADEDNESS, SHORTNESS OF BREATH, CHEST PAIN, OR ANY OTHER CONCERNING SYMPTOMS, DISCONTINUE IMMEDIATELY AND SEEK GUIDANCE FROM A QUALIFIED MEDICAL PROFESSIONAL BEFORE CONTINUING.**

## Step 4: Mindful Inhalation

- Light the cigarette slowly and deliberately.
- Take one or two deep puffs and cough it up.
- Instead of numbing out, pay close attention to the harshness of the smoke, the bitterness of the taste, the irritation in your throat and lungs.
- Blow smoke into a tissue or handkerchief. Notice the discoloration it leaves behind.

## Step 5: Immediate Replacement

- Put the cigarette down in an ashtray or somewhere safe.
- Pick up your cinnamon stick, coffee stirrer, or straw.
- Take three to five deep breaths through it, filling your lungs with clean air.
- Notice the contrast: the fresh oxygen soothes you while the cigarette harms you.

## Step 6: Repeat the Cycle

- Go back to Steps 4 and 5 and complete them two more times.
- When finished with your aversion session, extinguish the cigarette in your jar of water.

- Place each used cigarette in the jar of water. At the end of every session, take a brief sniff to reinforce just how foul and disgusting cigarettes really are. Return to the jar any time you need a quick reminder.

### Step 7: Journal Reflection

- Write down exactly what you experienced.
- Be honest about the taste, the smell, and the feelings.
- Reinforce the truth: *"Cigarettes are not my comfort. They are my poison."*

## ☐ 2. MOVEMENT RESET (Optional but Powerful)

- Take a 5-minute "freedom walk."
- Inhale clean air through your nose, exhale slowly through your mouth.
- Say in your head: "This is what calm really feels like."

## ☐ 3. CRAVING LEVEL (Before/After)

Record in your journal:

- **Before Session:** ____/10
- **After Session:** ____/10
- **Disgust Level:** ____/10

## ☐ 4. ACCOUNTABILITY STEP

- Text your partner: "Day 1: Done."

## ☐ 5. SCRIPT FOR THE DAY

- *"The illusion is breaking. Oxygen, not nicotine, is my calm."*

# DAY 1 REFLECTION

You just faced your habit without hiding. That's courage, not weakness. You didn't cave. You studied the craving. You looked it in the eye and saw it for what it is: a parasite that only lives if you feed it.

If you feel strange or restless right now, that's not failure—that's withdrawal. That's your brain rewiring itself toward freedom. You may also feel your concentration dip, your patience shrink, or your appetite spike. These changes are temporary chemical echoes of nicotine leaving your blood. Your body is already stabilizing its oxygen levels. Within 24 hours, your blood pressure and heart rate begin to normalize.

Write one more sentence in your journal: "*I did something hard today, and I didn't flinch.*"

You've already started breaking the spell.

## SUPPORT YOUR BODY AS IT HEALS

Your body is working hard to detox and rebalance. You can help it by giving it the fuel it needs to repair and regulate.

Simple nutrients and foods that support withdrawal:

- **Vitamin C:** Cigarettes drain it faster than almost any nutrient. Rebuild it with oranges, kiwis, strawberries, or a 500–1000 mg supplement.
- **B Vitamins (especially B6 and B12):** Help restore mood and energy as dopamine levels stabilize. Found in eggs, chicken, salmon, fortified cereals, or a basic B-complex vitamin.
- **Magnesium:** Calms muscle tension and helps with irritability. Try almonds, spinach, pumpkin seeds, or a 250–400 mg supplement before bed.
- **Omega-3 fatty acids:** Reduce inflammation and help repair cell membranes damaged by smoke. Eat salmon, walnuts, avocados, or flaxseed oil.
- **Protein snacks:** Nicotine once suppressed your appetite. Protein helps stabilize blood sugar and reduce the urge to "graze." Keep hard-boiled eggs, yogurt, or nuts nearby.
- **Hydration:** Water is the cheapest detox. Aim for at least eight glasses a day. Add lemon or cucumber slices to make it more enjoyable.

Avoid for now:

- **Excess caffeine (can intensify jitters)**
- **Excess sugar (spikes and crashes mimic cravings)**
- **Alcohol/other drugs (lowers inhibition and increases relapse risk)**

Every healthy bite and sip is a signal to your body that the healing has begun.

## DAY 2

**MISSION:** Repeat the aversion. Reinforce the truth. Crack the craving's illusion wide open.

### DAILY CHECKLIST

☐ 1. SCHEDULED AVERSION SESSION (Same time as yesterday)

- Go to your inconvenient stash location.
- Mirror. Light up.
- Take 1–2 mindful puffs—or until you feel the disgust building—and cough. Stop when you arrive at Destination Disgust.
- Speak the truth aloud as you smoke:
- "You don't comfort me, oxygen does."
- "You control me, but not for long. I am taking back control of my life"
- Focus on how automatic the motions feel—the reach, the light, the inhale.
- Now realize: you can interrupt any of it.
- Drop the butt/pod into the jar. Watch it die.
- Switch to 4-7-8 breathing immediately.

☐ **JOURNAL:** "What's different between yesterday's smoke/vape and today's?"

☐ **2. REPLACEMENT DRILL #1 — Hydration Cue**

- Pour a glass of water.
- Take a slow sip every time a craving hits.
- Think: "Clean in, clean out."
- When the urge hits, use the 4-7-8 or "Hee Hee" breathing technique.

☐ **3. MOVEMENT RESET**

- Walk for 5 minutes, just like yesterday.
- Stretch arms wide, open your chest.
- Remind yourself: "My lungs belong to me again."

☐ **4. CRAVING LEVEL (Before/After)**

- Before Session: ____/10
- After Session: ____/10
- Disgust Level: ____/10

☐ **5. ACCOUNTABILITY STEP**

Text your partner: "Day 2: Spell's cracking."

☐ **6. SCRIPT FOR THE DAY**: "Nicotine lies. Oxygen tells the truth."

# DAY 2 REFLECTION

By now, you've seen it: smoking doesn't calm you—breathing does.

Today wasn't about cutting down; it was about cutting through the illusion.

Each time you said the words out loud, you weakened nicotine's grip on your subconscious. That's how rewiring happens, through repetition and awareness.

You've completed two days. You're already halfway to physical freedom. Physically, this is the peak of withdrawal. Cravings may surge and your mood may swing. That's the nicotine receptors in your brain recalibrating to life without constant stimulation. When it hits, drink water, move your body, or breathe until the wave passes. Most cravings last only two to five minutes. Ride it out; every wave ends in calm.

Write one more line in your journal tonight: *"I see the trap. I choose the exit."*

# DAY 3

**MISSION:** Expose the last of nicotine's lies. Replace false comfort with real control.

## DAILY CHECKLIST

☐ **1. SCHEDULED AVERSION SESSION (same time as always)**

- Go to your inconvenient stash location.
- Stand in front of the mirror.
- Light your cigarette or vape, take 1–2 mindful puffs—or until your body says, "Enough." Make sure you reach Destination Disgust.
- As you smoke, say out loud:
- "You never calmed me, you caged me."
- Notice the disconnect between what you think you feel (relief) and what's actually happening (tightness, heat, bitterness).
- Drop the butt or pod into the jar of water. Watch it hiss and die.
- Immediately step outside for a 5-minute Freedom Walk.
- Inhale fresh air deeply.
- Say quietly, "This is what real relief feels like."
- Do 3 rounds of 4-7-8 breathing.

☐   **JOURNAL:** "What sensations did I feel while smoking? What sensations did I feel while breathing?"

☐   **2. MOVEMENT DRILL—Freedom Walk (5 min)**

- Done immediately after your aversion session.
- Focus on your posture — stand tall, chest open. You're physically reclaiming your body.

☐   **3. REPLACEMENT DRILL — Straw or Cinnamon Stick**

- Keep it in your pocket.
- When the hand-to-mouth urge hits, mimic the motion using the stick.
- Each time, say internally: "Control restored."

☐   **4. CRAVING LEVEL (Before/After)**

- **Before Session: ____/10**
- **After Session: ____/10**
- **Disgust Level: ____/10**

☐   **5. ACCOUNTABILITY STEP**

- Text your partner: "Day 3: Illusion's collapsing."

☐   **6. SCRIPT FOR THE DAY**

- "I'm not craving. I'm cleansing my body, my mind, and my spirit."

# DAY 3 REFLECTION

You're over the halfway mark. Your body is already purging nicotine. Your taste buds, circulation, and oxygen levels are changing—literally rewiring in real time.

By now, most of the nicotine is gone from your bloodstream. What remains are mental triggers—routines and emotions your brain still links to smoking. This is why today can feel both freeing and frustrating. The good news? Physical withdrawal is mostly behind you. From here on, it's mindset, not chemistry, that wins.

If you felt restless today, that's the illusion collapsing. Addiction tries to fight hardest right before it loses.

Tonight, write this in your journal: ***"The craving is a lie. I know what freedom feels like."***

You're not quitting anymore, you're transforming.

# DAY 4

**MISSION:** Let the feeling of disgust do the heavy lifting. You're almost free.

## DAILY CHECKLIST

☐ **1. SCHEDULED AVERSION SESSION (Same time)**

- Go to your inconvenient stash location.
- Mirror. Light.
- Take 1 puff and stop—or continue until you've reached Destination Disgust.
- Focus on the contrast:
- The bitter taste vs. the memory of clean air.
- The stale smell vs. the scent of your skin, clothes, or room.
- The burn in your throat vs. the calm of 4-7-8 breathing.
- Say out loud:
- "This isn't pleasure. This is poison."
- Drop the butt or pod into the jar of water. Watch it drown.
- Rinse your mouth or brush your teeth immediately.
- Breathe clean for one full minute.

☐ **JOURNAL:** "What moment today triggered disgust? Describe it."

☐ **2. REPLACEMENT DRILL—Taste Reset**

- After each craving, sip cold water or chew mint gum.
- Feel the freshness. Reinforce the association: clean > smoke.

☐ **3. REFLECTION EXERCISE—Gratitude List**

- Write 3 things you've gained in the past 4 days.
- Examples: better breathing, fewer excuses, control, pride.

☐ **4. CRAVING LEVEL (Before/After)**

- **Before Session: ____/10**

- After Session: ____/10
- Disgust Level: ____/10

## ☐ 5. ACCOUNTABILITY STEP

- Text your partner: "Day 4: Disgust is setting in."

## ☐ 6. SCRIPT FOR THE DAY

- "This isn't comfort. It's decay. I choose clean."

## DAY 4 REFLECTION

You're nearly there. The Aversion Sessions are breaking the bond between nicotine and reward.

Most people can barely finish a puff on Day 4. That's victory. That's your body reclaiming its boundaries.

Write this line before bed: *"Tomorrow, I say goodbye."*

# DAY 5

MISSION: End the story for good. Create your final, lasting memory of disgust and freedom.

## DAILY CHECKLIST

## ☐ 1. SCHEDULED AVERSION SESSION (Final Session)

- Go to your inconvenient stash location.
- Stand in front of the mirror. Look yourself in the eyes.
- Light a cigarette or vape.
- For your Grand Finale cigarette, inhale and cough it up until your chest feels raw. This is your final chainlink that you break—one that will leave a very strong, immersive memory of your final goodbye. Take your final mindful, very harsh puffs. Remember to inhale and cough them up until you get to your final Destination Disgust.
- Look at yourself in the mirror and truly see what nicotine has done.
- Study your reflection.
- See the yellowing of your teeth, the dullness in your skin, the wrinkles that came long before their time.
- Look at your fingertips — the faint stains that no soap can fully remove.

- Notice the tiredness in your eyes, the tightness in your chest, the way smoke has slowly written itself onto your face.

This is your final picture of who nicotine made you. And this is the last time you'll ever see that version of yourself again.

Say goodbye out loud. Speak to the addiction directly. Don't mumble. Don't whisper. Say it clearly, looking yourself dead in the eyes:

- "Goodbye. You no longer control me."
- "The mind is like a recorder. The last memory in is the last memory out. My last memory is disgust."

Let the sound of your voice cut through the silence. That's you reclaiming authority. That's the voice of your free mind overriding the whispers of addiction.

Drop it into the water jar. Watch and listen as it hisses and dies. Destroy the rest: crush, toss, delete, uninstall. Throw out the glass jar or keep it sealed as a reminder—your "Freedom Trophy."

Do 3 rounds of 4-7-8 breathing.

☐ JOURNAL:

- "This was my last cigarette."
- "This was my last chain."
- "This was my freedom moment."

## ☐ 2. FREEDOM RITUAL (Optional but Powerful)

- Wash your hands thoroughly, physically removing the residue.
- Light a candle or incense to mark the new chapter.
- Say out loud: "*I don't smoke. I KICKED IT.*"

## ☐ 3. CELEBRATE COMPLETION

- Go to KickItStopSmoking.com/Diploma.
- Download the Cold Turkey Program Diploma.
- Print it, sign it, frame it, or snap a picture with it.

This is your badge of courage, proof that you didn't just think about change. You make it happen.

☐ **4. CRAVING LEVEL (Before/After)**

- **Before Session:** ____/10
- **After Session:** ____/10
- **Disgust Level:** ____/10

☐ **5. ACCOUNTABILITY STEP**

- Text your partner: "Day 5: I KICKED IT."

# DAY 5 REFLECTION:
# THE GOOD-BYE LETTER

Write one final entry in your journal: "*I release this habit. It no longer defines me. My body is mine. My breath is mine. I am free.*"

If emotion hits you today, let it. That's your body and brain celebrating their reunion. The chains aren't loosening anymore. They're gone.

# CLAIM YOUR KICK IT DIPLOMA

Before you move forward, take a moment to acknowledge what you've done.

Go to KickItDr.Judy.com/Diploma and download your Cold Turkey Program Diploma.

Print it. Sign it. Date it. Frame it or post it somewhere visible—your mirror, your desk, your fridge.

This isn't vanity, it's evidence. Every glance at that diploma reminds you: You didn't taper off. You didn't hesitate. You faced the illusion and crushed it in five days flat.

You didn't just think about change. You KICKED IT.

# FIVE DAYS THAT CHANGED EVERYTHING

Pause for a moment and consider what you just did.

Five days ago, nicotine was running your life. It dictated when you took breaks. It decided whether you could focus. It controlled your mood, your rituals, your identity. The chains on the cover of this book? They were wrapped around you so tightly you couldn't see where you ended and the addiction began.

And in five days—just five—you shattered every link.

That's not willpower. That's transformation.

The cold turkey approach demands everything at once. There's no easing in, no soft landings. You face the full weight of withdrawal, the complete collapse of old routines, the raw exposure of every emotional trigger—all in a concentrated burst. Most people never attempt it. Those who do often fail.

But you didn't just attempt it. You completed it.

And something has changed inside you because of it.

## THE SHIFT THAT'S ALREADY HAPPENING

In my clinical practice, I've observed that cold turkey quitters often experience the paradigm shift more suddenly than those who quit gradually. The intensity of the five-day protocol creates a kind of psychological breaking point where the old identity can't hold anymore.

You may have already felt it:

- A moment during Day 3 or 4 when you realized the craving wasn't as strong as your conviction.
- The strange sensation on Day 5 of looking at your last cigarette with something close to pity—not longing.
- A clarity in your thinking that feels unfamiliar, like fog lifting after years of haze.
- The first deep breath that felt like it actually reached the bottom of your lungs.

These experiences aren't just symptoms of nicotine leaving your bloodstream. They're evidence that your brain is rewiring in real time. Your neural pathways are literally changing, building new connections that support who you're becoming instead of who you were.

## FROM DISGUST TO IDENTITY

You've reached Destination Disgust. That's the foundation. But disgust alone won't carry you for the rest of your life—you need something stronger.

You need a new identity.

Right now, you might still think of yourself as "a smoker who quit." That's natural after five days. But there's a profound difference between someone who is constantly resisting cigarettes and someone who simply doesn't smoke. The first person lives in perpetual battle. The second person is free.

The paradigm shift is what moves you from the first category to the second. It's the moment when cigarettes stop making sense—not because you're fighting them, but because they no longer fit who you are.

That shift is closer than you think. Some people experience it as a single flash of insight. Others feel it as a gradual dawning. Either way, Chapter 10 will help you recognize it, embrace it, and build on it.

## WHAT COMES NEXT

The intensity of these five days has broken nicotine's physical grip on you. But lasting freedom requires more than breaking chains—it requires building a life where those chains can never reattach.

In the next chapter, you'll learn how the paradigm shift transforms your relationship not just with cigarettes, but with yourself. You'll discover how to encode your new identity so deeply that smoking becomes genuinely unthinkable—not because you're resisting temptation, but because the old you no longer exists.

You'll also see how this transformation ripples outward—into your relationships, your work, your role in your family and community. The freedom you've claimed isn't just personal. It's generational.

## BEFORE YOU CONTINUE

Take your journal and write today's date at the top of a fresh page. Then write:

- *"I completed the 5-Day Cold Turkey Aversion Plan. I reached Destination Disgust. The chains are broken. Now I'm ready to become who I was always meant to be."*
- **Sign it with your full name.**

You didn't just survive these five days. You transformed through them. The hardest part is complete. What follows isn't another battle, but an awakening.

Chapter 10 will show you how to secure this freedom for the rest of your life. Turn the page when you're ready.

You've earned what comes next.

# CHAPTER 10.

## THE PARADIGM SHIFT
### Living In The Light of Your New Identity

> **And then the day came when the risk to remain tight in a bud was more painful than the risk it took to blossom.**
>
> – Anaïs Nin

# LOOK AT HOW FAR YOU'VE COME

Take a moment and breathe this in: you've done something extraordinary.

You've faced wounds that were buried for years. You've dismantled the defenses that once felt like armor. You've exposed cigarettes for what they are—liars, manipulators, thieves. You've chosen honesty when illusions would have been easier.

Most people never get this far. They keep hiding behind their defenses, clutching cigarettes like a security blanket. But not you. You've walked through the hardest work already. And now, something is beginning to happen inside you.

This chapter is about the moment when the shift takes hold. It's not about gritting your teeth anymore. It's about becoming someone new.

# SIGNS OF THE PARADIGM SHIFT

You'll know the shift is happening because cigarettes start to lose their spell over you. Not in theory, but in ways you feel every day.

- You catch yourself laughing with your child and realize you haven't thought about smoking in hours.
- You walk past a smoker and, instead of longing, you feel relief that it isn't you anymore.
- Think back on an aversion session and find the thought revolting—something inside you no longer wants it.
- You feel calmer after a deep breath, and you finally understand the calm was yours all along.
- You begin thinking, "I don't smoke," instead of, "I'm trying not to smoke."

These are not small changes. They are seismic. They are the signs that your identity is shifting at the deepest level.

# PANEL 7 – THE PARADIGM SHIFT

In the Mind Map, **Panel 7** is the moment of awakening. It's the turning point when everything you've been working toward clicks into place.

Some patients describe it as an Ah-ha! experience—sudden, shocking, undeniable. For others, it arrives like dawn—gradual, gentle, but unstoppable. Either way, the moment is unforgettable.

## MARCUS'S AWAKENING

For Marcus, the ER nurse, the shift happened in the middle of a trauma case. He was fully present, focused, and steady. Hours passed before he realized he hadn't thought once about smoking. "It hit me," he said later. "All this time, I thought cigarettes gave me control. But it was me. I was the one who kept showing up strong. I always had that inside me."

## JENNIFER'S FREEDOM

Jennifer's moment was quieter but just as powerful. She had quit smoking for weeks, but still felt haunted by cravings. Then one evening, she tucked her daughter into bed. Her daughter hugged her tightly and whispered, "Mommy, you smell like shampoo instead of smoke."

Jennifer told me later, "I cried that night. For the first time, I realized I wasn't depriving myself anymore—I was giving my daughter a gift. I never want to go back."

## SHOSHANNAH'S CONFIDENCE

For Shoshannah, the marketing creative, the shift came at a networking event. She used to rely on cigarettes and then her vape pens to feel polished and confident. But this time, she walked in, greeted colleagues, and realized she felt comfortable in her own skin. "It wasn't me plus a vape anymore," she said. "It was just me. And that was enough."

This is the paradigm shift. The illusion collapses, and the truth rushes in: you never needed cigarettes to begin with.

**They never gave you comfort.**
**You created comfort.**

**They never gave you control.**
**You were the steady one all along.**

**They never gave you confidence.**
**You carried it inside yourself..**

# PANEL 8 – NEW ENCODING

Once the paradigm shift takes hold, something remarkable begins: your inner wiring starts to change.

The old beliefs that once trapped you—*"I can't cope without cigarettes," "I need them to manage stress," "I can't be myself without smoking"*—begin to fade. In their place, new beliefs, emotions, and behaviors take root.

I call this new encoding. It's the stage where you stop rehearsing freedom and begin living it.

## FOUR PILLARS OF NEW ENCODING

### BELIEFS:

- Old: "I can't handle stress without cigarettes."
- New: "I can handle life directly. I have healthier tools."

### EMOTIONS:

- Old: "I need to numb feelings."
- New: "I can let myself feel and still be safe."

### BEHAVIORS:

- Old: "I take a smoke break."
- New: "I take a breathing break, a walk, or a stretch."

### RELATIONSHIPS:

- Old: "I hide my smoking from others."
- New: "I connect openly, without shame or secrecy."

## JENNIFER'S REWIRING

Jennifer used to smoke when she felt invisible. Now, she calls a friend. "I thought cigarettes made me feel cared for," she told me, "but it turns out real connection feels even better."

This is what new encoding feels like: replacing false comfort with real care, false control with true calm, false confidence with authentic self-worth.

## PANEL 9 – UNITY AND SERVICE

The final stage of the Mind Map™ is integration. You're no longer a smoker in recovery—you're simply someone who doesn't smoke.

But more than that, you begin to feel the ripple effect of your transformation. Healing yourself creates space to help others.

- Parents model resilience to their children.

- Nurses and teachers inspire colleagues.
- Friends quietly encourage each other: "If they can do it, maybe I can too."

Healing never stops with the individual. It spreads outward into families, workplaces, communities, and even across generations.

## MARCUS'S LEGACY

Eight months after quitting, Marcus wasn't just smoke-free—he was mentoring new nurses. "I tell them, don't rely on unhealthy habits to get through the stress. Take care of yourself first. That's how you last in this work."

## THE RIPPLE

Every time you say no to a cigarette, you say yes to life—not just for yourself, but for everyone who depends on you. Children, partners, colleagues, and even strangers absorb the energy of your freedom.

This is Panel 9: unity and service. It's not about being perfect. It's about living authentically and letting your healing ripple outward.

## THE NEUROSCIENCE OF IDENTITY CHANGE

This transformation is more than psychological—it's biological as well.

Your brain is wired through experience. For years, you strengthened the "smoking pathways," teaching your brain that nicotine was essential. That's why cigarettes felt irresistible.

But your brain is also plastic—it can change at any age. This is called neuroplasticity. Every time you choose clean air over smoke, you strengthen new neural pathways. Every time you breathe instead of light up, you reinforce your new identity.

At first, it takes effort. But with repetition, the new pathways grow stronger, while the old smoking pathways weaken from disuse.

Science proves what you're experiencing: the more you live as a non-smoker, the more natural it becomes.

## A MESSAGE OF HOPE

Here's what I want you to know: relapse doesn't erase your new wiring. It simply means the old circuit flickered. Every time you return to your tools, you strengthen freedom again.

Your brain is learning. Your identity is shifting. Every moment of practice writes the story of who you are becoming.

# LIVING THE SHIFT

By now, you've crossed into new territory. You're not just surviving without cigarettes, you're thriving in freedom.

Living the shift means weaving your new identity into daily life. It's not about perfection. It's about practicing authenticity, day after day, until it feels natural.

## DAILY PRACTICES FOR LIVING THE SHIFT:

- **Keep a Freedom Journal.** Record victories, big or small. Write about the walk you enjoyed without wheezing, the hug you shared without smelling like smoke, the clarity of a morning unclouded by nicotine.
- **Celebrate Milestones.** One week, one month, three months—acknowledge them. Treat yourself to a reward that feels meaningful.
- **Use Truth Affirmations.** Repeat to yourself:
  - "I am free."
  - "My body is healing."
  - "I am not a smoker. I am a whole, authentic person."
- **Share Your Story.** Tell a friend, a family member, or a coworker about your transformation. Speaking it out loud strengthens your identity and gives others hope.

# THE EMOTIONAL PAYOFF

Freedom isn't just about better breathing or saving money. It's about reclaiming moments you didn't know you were losing.

- A child leaning in close without pulling back from the smell.
- A long walk where your chest feels light.
- A conversation where you're fully present, not distracted by the itch of craving.
- The pride in knowing you faced something hard and won.

These are the treasures of the shift. They are the evidence that the cigarette never gave you life. It only stole it.

# CLOSING MESSAGE

As your guide on this journey, I want to pause here and speak to you directly.

You have done something rare and remarkable. You've chosen healing over illusion, courage over fear, truth over deception. You've faced the hardest parts of yourself and chosen freedom.

You are not the same person who picked up this book.

That person was trapped in the Double Dungeon, convinced the doors were locked. You've discovered the truth that those doors were never locked at all. You've walked through them into light, authenticity, and wholeness.

Carry this truth with you. You don't need cigarettes. You never did. What you needed was comfort, safety, and confidence—and those were inside you all along.

# PREPARING FOR CHAPTER 11

This isn't the end of your journey. It's the beginning of a new one. You are free today, but freedom must be protected. Life will still bring stress, loss, and temptation. Old defenses may try to return. The cigarette may whisper again.

That's why the next chapter matters.

In Chapter 11, we'll talk about relapse, not as failure, but as part of the human experience. You'll learn how to respond if you slip, how to recover quickly, and how to turn setbacks into strength.

Because freedom isn't fragile. It's resilient. And so are you.

# CHAPTER 11.

## WHEN THE DOUBLE DUNGEON RETURNS
### Relapse, Recovery, and Protecting Your Freedom

" **Fall seven times and stand up eight.** "

– Japanese Proverb

# RELAPSE IS NOT FAILURE

Let me say this as clearly as I can: relapse is not failure.

If you slip and smoke again, it doesn't erase your progress. It doesn't mean you're weak. It doesn't mean everything you've done until now was wasted. It simply means there is more healing to do.

Relapse is not a collapse of character—it is information. It is your body and mind signaling that a wound or trigger still needs attention.

What matters is not whether you slip. What matters is how quickly and compassionately you recover.

## WHY RELAPSE HAPPENS

Relapse can be triggered by many things:

- Stress: Work deadlines, conflict at home, financial pressure.
- Loss: Grief, heartbreak, or disappointment.
- Celebrations: Weddings, reunions, or nights out with friends.
- Loneliness: Feeling unseen or unsupported.
- Old environments: Being around smokers or revisiting places tied to smoking.

Sometimes relapse happens in obvious moments of stress. Other times, it sneaks in during joy or nostalgia. A smell, a memory, or a social cue can bring back the illusion of comfort in an instant.

But remember: relapse doesn't mean you're back at the beginning. Even if you smoke again, you are wiser than before. You have tools, awareness, and strength you didn't have when you first picked up this book.

## TYPES OF RELAPSE

In my clinical work, I've seen two main types of relapse:

### 1. IMPLEMENTATION RELAPSE

- Happens before the paradigm shift fully takes hold.
- Usually occurs in the first days or weeks of quitting.
- Driven by defenses: "Just one won't hurt."

- Feels discouraging, but recovery is possible with structure.

## 2. POST-SHIFT RELAPSE

- Happens after the paradigm shift and identity shift have begun.
- Usually triggered by stress, grief, or unexpected situations.
- The difference: it feels wrong. Most people report the cigarette tastes terrible or feels unnatural.
- Easier to recover from because the new identity is already forming.

# A CASE STORY: GILBERT'S RELAPSE

I'll never forget a story shared with me by the father of one of my former assistants. His name was Gilbert, and his experience is a vivid reminder of how quickly relapse can take hold.

Relapse doesn't always come with a dramatic buildup. Sometimes, it's just one moment, one choice, one puff.

Gilbert started smoking at fourteen. By the time he was twenty-six, he had already been a smoker for twelve years—through high school, through Vietnam, through the chaos of early adulthood. When he finally returned home, determined to rebuild his life, he quit.

He told himself, "I'm going to be back. I'm going to go to school. I'm going to get my life right. I will not be addicted to cigarettes anymore." And for a while, he succeeded. He hadn't smoked a single cigarette since coming back from Vietnam.

One day, while using the GI Bill to study at Cal State Northridge, he sat in the back of a lecture hall. Next to him, a girl opened a pack of cigarettes. She lit one, and the smoke drifted into the air.

The moment Gilbert smelled it, something inside him stirred. The scent was familiar. It was warm. It was pleasing. It reminded him of all the "joys" he once associated with smoking—the false comfort, the social ease, the identity.

Without overthinking, he turned to the girl, gathered his nerve, and asked, "May I have one of those?"

She smiled, said "Sure," and handed him one without hesitation. And just like that, after months of being smoke-free, Gilbert relapsed.

He couldn't believe how easy it was. One puff was all it took to restart the cycle. That one cigarette turned into another eight years of smoking.

# THE MORAL OF THE STORY

Relapse isn't just a puff. It's not harmless. For many, it's a doorway back into years of addiction. That's why commitment matters. That's why protecting your freedom matters.

The lesson from Gilbert's story is clear: ***ONE PUFF RE-ADDICTS.***

But why?

It's not because one puff is enough to chemically re-addict you to nicotine. Chemically, a single cigarette isn't sufficient to hook your body again. The real danger is psychological.

That one puff is enough to *reinforce the thousands of urges it took for you to reach it.* Each urge you resisted builds tension, and when you finally give in, the "relief" you feel doesn't just reinforce the puff, it reinforces *every single urge* that led up to it.

This is what psychologists call intermittent reinforcement, the most powerful reinforcement schedule discovered in behavioral psychology.

B.F. Skinner demonstrated this in his classic experiments. Rats were trained to press a lever to receive food pellets. At first, every press released food. Then Skinner stopped the pellets entirely—a process called extinction. The rats eventually slowed down, pressing less when nothing happened.

But then, after all hope of another pull of the lever producing food was lost, Skinner let a single pellet drop. Instantly, the rats went wild, pressing the lever frantically. That one pellet reignited the behavior as if extinction had never happened.

The brain doesn't forget the pathway. It simply lies dormant, waiting for a trigger. Nicotine works the same way. One puff is enough to reactivate the conditioned association and reopen the old wiring, pulling you back into the cycle as if you had never quit.

That doesn't mean relapse is the end. But it does mean the stakes are high. Once you've chosen freedom, you must protect it with vigilance.

Relapse prevention isn't about living in fear. Instead, it's about living with awareness. It's about remembering that every cigarette carries the potential to pull you back into the Double Dungeon, and choosing instead to stay in the light.

# THE RAPID RECOVERY PROTOCOL

Relapse can feel like a tidal wave of shame. But shame keeps you stuck instead of helping you recover. What you need is a clear, compassionate roadmap back to freedom. That's what the Rapid Recovery Protocol is for.

Follow these steps immediately after a relapse:

### 1. STOP THE SHAME SPIRAL.

- Take a deep breath.
- Say to yourself: "This slip does not erase my progress. I am still on the path to freedom."

### 2. ASSESS THE TRIGGER.

- Ask: "What just happened? What thought, feeling, or situation made me reach for a cigarette?"
- Write it down in your journal. Clarity turns shame into knowledge.

### 3. RECONNECT TO THE MIND MAP.

- Identify where you got stuck. Was it Chaos (Panel 4)? Defenses (Panel 5)? The Breakdown point (Panel 6)?
- Remember: awareness gives you leverage.

### 4. RE-ENGAGE AVERSION THERAPY.

- Perform one session immediately.
- Face the cigarette in the mirror. Remind yourself of its harsh taste and foul smell. Replace it with clean breathing.

### 5. REACH OUT FOR SUPPORT.

- Text or call your accountability partner.
- Say honestly: "I slipped, but I'm back on track."
- Let someone remind you that you're not alone.

### 6. RECOMMIT IMMEDIATELY.

- Do not wait for "next week" or "after the weekend."
- Set your quit date again—today. Right now.
- Say it out loud: "I recommit to my freedom."

# WHY THIS PROTOCOL WORKS

Relapse only has lasting power if you hide it, deny it, or drown in shame. When you shine light on it immediately, it loses its grip.

Think of relapse not as a collapse but as a flare pointing to where more healing is needed. The Rapid Recovery Protocol lets you respond with strength instead of self-blame.

### SHORT-TERM RECOVERY: THE FIRST WEEK AFTER RELAPSE

The days right after a relapse are critical. Here's how to stabilize quickly:

- **Aversion Therapy:** Do 1–2 sessions daily. Rebuild the disgust connection.
- **Breathing Practices:** Use the 4-7-8 or Hee-Hee breathing when cravings hit.
- **Nutrition:** Load up on Vitamin C, B-complex, magnesium, and hydration. These support your nervous system during re-stabilization.
- **Journaling:** Write morning and evening reflections. Ask: "What did I learn today about my triggers and my strength?"
- **Support:** Check in daily with your accountability partner. Share both victories and struggles.

Within a week, most patients feel back on track, often stronger than before. The relapse becomes part of their story of resilience.

# CASE STUDY: ALICIA'S BOUNCE-BACK

Alicia, a 39-year-old single mother, quit smoking through the Five-Day Aversion Plan. For three months she was free. Then one night, after a draining day at work and a heated argument with her ex-partner, she caved.

"I was so angry," she told me. "I drove to the gas station, bought a pack, and smoked one in the car. I felt terrible the moment I did it. It didn't even taste good. But I felt like I had blown everything."

Instead of hiding it, Alicia used the Rapid Recovery Protocol. She journaled what happened, performed an aversion session that same night, and texted her sister: "I slipped, but I'm not giving up."

The next morning, she woke up smoke-free again. She spent the week doubling down on breathing techniques, calling her accountability partner daily, and writing in her journal.

By the end of that week, she felt stronger than before. "I realized one cigarette doesn't erase my freedom," she said. "What mattered was what I did next."

## THE LESSON

Relapse isn't the end unless you let it be. Alicia's story proves what I tell every patient: the fastest way back to freedom is immediate recommitment.

The cigarette may whisper, "You've failed, you might as well keep smoking." But the truth is the opposite: you are stronger now, because you've faced the cigarette's lie and chosen to stand up again.

## LONG-TERM PROTECTION

Once you've recovered from a relapse, the next step is protecting your freedom for the long run. Freedom isn't fragile—but it does require attention. Think of it like a garden: you've planted new seeds, but weeds can grow back if you stop tending to it.

Here are strategies to keep your progress strong:

- **Keep Growing.** Don't stagnate once you quit. Explore new hobbies, exercise, or personal growth work. Expansion keeps your brain building healthy pathways instead of longing for old ones.
- **Stay Connected.** Isolation breeds relapse. Maintain ties with your accountability partner, support group, or trusted friends. Connection is the antidote to the loneliness that often triggers smoking.
- **Expect Challenges.** Holidays, stressful seasons, grief, or even celebrations can test you. Anticipating them lets you prepare in advance rather than being blindsided.
- **Anchor Milestones.** Celebrate every achievement—one month, six months, a year. Mark them with rituals that reinforce pride in your smoke-free identity.

Long-term protection isn't about fear. It's about stewardship of your freedom.

## PANEL 9 IN ACTION: SERVICE AND LEGACY

The final panel of the Mind Map is unity and service. Relapse prevention becomes strongest when you stop making your healing only about you. When you share your story, help others, or model freedom for your family, your identity as a non-smoker becomes unshakable.

- **Parents inspire children.** Kids learn resilience when they see a parent break the cycle.
- **Workers inspire colleagues.** Smoke-free employees often become quiet mentors in

their workplace.

- **Communities ripple.** Each person who heals makes it easier for the next to believe freedom is possible.

Every time you tell someone, "I used to smoke, but I don't anymore," you anchor that truth deeper in yourself. And you give hope to someone still struggling.

# SARAH'S FULL CIRCLE

Remember Sarah, from Chapter 1? The successful executive whose daughter once called her a hypocrite? Months into her smoke-free life, Sarah experienced a scare.

She was at a dinner party when someone offered her a cigarette. For a split second, the old defenses rose up: "One won't hurt. I've been doing so well."

But instead of taking it, she paused. She thought of her daughter's words. She remembered the journal entry where she admitted, "Cigarettes are controlling me, and I hate that." She pictured the aversion session when she saw her reflection clouded in smoke.

Then she said, "No thank you. I don't smoke anymore."

Later she told me, "I was shocked by how good that felt. Saying no wasn't deprivation—it was pride. My daughter noticed too. She said, 'Mom, you don't sneak outside anymore.' That meant everything."

Sarah's story shows the power of full circle. Even when tempted, she chose truth. And each time she did, her identity as a non-smoker grew stronger.

# CLOSING: RESILIENT FREEDOM

Relapse may happen. Triggers may whisper. Defenses may try to sneak back in. But here's what you must remember: freedom is not fragile. It is resilient.

Every time you resist a cigarette, you reinforce your new identity. Every time you bounce back after a slip, you grow stronger. Every time you share your story, you extend your healing to others.

You are not the same person who began this journey. You are wiser, freer, more authentic. The Double Dungeon no longer defines you—you have the keys, and you know the way out.

In the next and final chapter, we'll reflect on your entire journey and the legacy you are creating. You'll see how your healing ripples across generations, becoming a gift far bigger than yourself.

# CHAPTER 12.

## LIVING YOUR LEGACY

### From Healing to Wholeness

> **What lies behind us and what lies before us are tiny matters compared to what lies within us.**
>
> – Ralph Waldo Emerson

# YOU HAVE DONE SOMETHING EXTRAORDINARY

Take a deep breath. Pause here. Let yourself feel what you've accomplished.

You have walked through a journey that most people never dare to face. You've looked at wounds buried deep in your past. You've dismantled defenses that once felt like your armor. You've faced the cigarette not as a friend but as the liar it always was. And you've chosen freedom.

This wasn't about willpower. It wasn't about gimmicks or shortcuts. It was about honesty. It was about healing the hole in your soul and rewriting the story you carried for years.

Most people spend a lifetime circling the same struggle. You chose something different. You chose truth. You chose wholeness. You chose life.

## THE JOURNEY YOU'VE TAKEN

Look back on the steps you've taken in these pages:

- You found your *why*—the reason powerful enough to carry you through cravings and doubt.
- You uncovered the hole in the soul, the wound that made cigarettes feel necessary.
- You faced your defenses—the rationalizations, the minimizations, the denials—and you chose honesty over illusion.
- You broke the cigarette's false romance with aversion therapy, forcing it to show its true face.
- You chose your path—Cold Turkey or Gradual Withdrawal—and followed through with courage.
- You endured the discomfort, and then you experienced the shift—the paradigm shift where smoking lost its power and freedom took root.
- You built new beliefs, new rituals, and new relationships as part of your new encoding.
- You learned how to protect your freedom, recover quickly if you slip, and ripple your healing into the lives of others.

This is the roadmap you've walked. This is the transformation you've earned.

### *You are NOT a smoker anymore.*

# LIVING THE NEW IDENTITY

Now comes the most beautiful part: living as someone who no longer smokes.

No more waking up with a cough and wondering when you'll have your first cigarette. No more calculating breaks, hiding smells or vape hits, or wondering if people notice. No more shame clouding the simple joys of life.

Instead, you breathe freely. You laugh without coughing. You hug your child or your partner without pulling back in embarrassment. You feel mornings unclouded by nicotine. You taste food more vividly, smell fresh air more deeply, and sense your own body healing day by day.

This is not about deprivation. It's about abundance. It's about reclaiming all the moments cigarettes once stole from you.

It's the joy of walking into a room and feeling whole.

It's the confidence of saying, "I don't smoke," without hesitation.

It's the peace of knowing you are free.

# DAILY ANCHORS FOR YOUR IDENTITY

To live the shift, you don't need perfection. You need practice. Here are simple anchors to reinforce your identity every day:

- **Freedom Journal:** Record victories, no matter how small. Write down when you felt proud, strong, or whole.
- **Milestone Celebrations:** Mark your progress—one week, one month, one year. Celebrate with rituals that honor your new life.
- **Truth Affirmations:** Remind yourself daily:
  - *"I am free."*
  - *"My body is healing."*
  - *"I am whole."*
- **Connection:** Share your story with someone. Each time you speak your truth, you strengthen it in yourself and offer hope to others.

# THE EMOTIONAL PAYOFF

Freedom isn't just measured in longer life or better health. It's measured in moments.

- The moment you realize you haven't thought about smoking all day.
- The moment your child notices you smell like fresh laundry instead of smoke.
- The moment you walk up stairs without gasping for breath.
- The moment you look in the mirror and see yourself—not a smoker, not an addict, but you.

These are the treasures cigarettes could never give you. These are the gifts of living your new identity.

## THE RIPPLE EFFECT AND YOUR LEGACY

Your decision to quit smoking doesn't end with you. It ripples outward, touching every life around you.

When you choose freedom, your children learn resilience. They see that cycles can be broken. They learn that stress can be faced directly, not hidden behind smoke. They inherit a healthier model for their own lives.

When you choose freedom, your spouse or partner feels your presence more deeply. You are there fully and authentically, without needing to sneak away.

When you choose freedom, your colleagues notice. You become an example of strength in your workplace. Even if you never speak about it, your actions inspire others.

Healing never stops with one person. It moves outward like waves in water. Each time you say "*I am free*", you make it easier for someone else to believe they can be free too.

This is your legacy—not just adding years to your life, but adding life to the years of everyone who looks to you for inspiration.

## A FINAL MESSAGE FROM MY HEART

If you were my patient, this is what I would say to you right now:

I am proud of you. Truly proud. You have faced wounds that most people spend a lifetime avoiding. You've taken cigarettes—the thing that once felt like your only comfort—and shown them for what they are: liars, thieves, abusers.

You've proven to yourself that freedom is possible.

You may still feel fear at times. That's okay. Fear means you're human. But you also have courage, and you've proven that courage is stronger.

If you slip, remember this: relapse is not failure. It's feedback. Use it to grow stronger. Pick yourself back up and recommit. Freedom is always waiting for you.

Above all, remember this truth: *you are not a smoker anymore*. You are whole, free, and authentic.

Carry this with you. Carry it into your family, your community, your world. Be The Cause—not just of your own healing, but of a ripple of healing that spreads far beyond you.

# ABOUT THE AUTHOR
## Dr. Judy Rosenberg

Dr. Judy Rosenberg, Ph.D. is a licensed clinical psychologist with over 40 years of experience helping people overcome addiction, trauma, and emotional wounds. She completed her undergraduate work in psychology at UCLA and earned her graduate degrees from the California Graduate Institute (CGI).

In 1980, she founded the original Habit Breakers Stop Smoking Clinic, pioneering an approach that addressed the deeper psychological roots of addiction. Her first book, *Dr. Judy's Habit Breakers Stop Smoking Plan*, sold over 250,000 copies. That clinical work evolved into the **Be The Cause Mind Map™ method**, a transformative nine-panel framework that has helped thousands of patients heal from the inside out.

Dr. Judy is the author of *Be The Cause®: Healing Human Disconnect*, the foundational book on her Mind Map approach to psychological healing as well as the critically renowned novel *Lucid Darkness*. She has appeared as a media psychologist on *MTV, E! Entertainment, CBS News, CNN,* and *Animal Planet,* and hosts the weekly call-in radio show *Dr. Judy WTF (What The Freud)!*

She is the founder of the **Psychological Healing Center**, where she has been in private practice since 1996. She sees patients in Sherman Oaks and Beverly Hills, California, as well as **via Telehealth**. Her mission is to help people break free from the patterns that keep them stuck, so they can Be The Cause® of their own healing.

### Continue Your Healing Journey
To learn more about Dr. Judy's Mind Map approach to psychological healing, read her book
*Be The Cause®: Healing Human Disconnect*, available wherever books are sold.

### Free Resources
Download your companion materials for this book—including the Stop Smoking Contract, printable Aversion Session guides, and more: www.kickitdrjudy.com

### Work with Dr. Judy
The Psychological Healing Center offers individual therapy, Telehealth sessions, and specialized programs for addiction recovery and trauma healing.
Sherman Oaks, California
www.psychologicalhealingcenter.com
310) 739-4491

**SCAN HERE**

www.ingramcontent.com/pod-product-compliance
Lightning Source LLC
Chambersburg PA
CBHW022136080426
42734CB00006B/389